READING LABELS
ON JAM TINS

BILL BUNBURY

All the major events in our history have been experienced at first-hand by ordinary Australians, who have lived to tell the tale. *Reading Labels on Jam Tins* captures a great many of the voices of those men and women — rural battlers, immigrants, Aborigines, housewives, prospectors, to name a few — who traditionally have remained unheard in the pages of histories.

Through a range of personal accounts of difficult times, each of the stories Bill Bunbury presents brings the reader into intimate contact with ordinary people whose life experiences are part of our history. Their memories vividly recreate stories that include the goldrushes, the Great Depression, the internment of Aboriginal children, and the pioneer life on the land and in the timber industry.

Based on his popular ABC social history radio programs, Bill Bunbury's *Reading Labels on Jam Tins* is a lively, highly readable collection of historical snapshots, in words and pictures.

Bill Bunbury is a producer with the ABC's Social History Unit, and is the presenter of 'Hindsight' each Sunday on Radio National. His other books include *Rag Sticks and Wire. Australians In the Air: Civil Aviation 1919-1980* (ABC Books, 1993), *Cyclone Tracy: Picking up the Pieces* (Fremantle Arts Centre Press, 1994), *Rabbits and Spaghetti: Captives and Comrades – Australians, Italians and the War 1934-1945* (Fremantle Arts Centre Press, 1995). He also co-wrote, with Ros Bowden, *Being Aboriginal* (Allen & Unwin, 1990).

Photograph courtesy ABC.

READING LABELS
ON JAM TINS

Wayside letterbox, Group Settlement.

READING LABELS ON JAM TINS

Living through Difficult Times

BILL BUNBURY

FREMANTLE ARTS CENTRE PRESS

First published 1993 by
FREMANTLE ARTS CENTRE PRESS
193 South Terrace (PO Box 320), South Fremantle
Western Australia 6162

Reprinted 1993, 1995.

Copyright © Bill Bunbury, 1993.

This book is copyright. Apart from any fair dealing for the purpose of private study,
research, criticism or review, as permitted under the Copyright Act, no part may be
reproduced by any process without written permission.
Enquiries should be made to the publisher.

Consultant Editor B R Coffey.
Picture Editor Helen Garwood.
Designed by John Douglass.
Production Coordinator Sue Chiera.

Typeset in Goudy Old-Style
by Fremantle Arts Centre Press
and printed on 115gsm Silk Matt
by Lamb Print, East Perth, WA

National Library of Australia
Cataloguing-in-publication data

Bunbury, Bill
Reading labels on jam tins.

ISBN 1 86368 031 4.

1. Oral history. 2. Western Australia — History — 20th century.
I. Title

994.104

Department for
theArts
Western Australia

Fremantle Arts Centre Press receives financial assistance from the
Western Australian Department for the Arts.

This book is dedicated to former forester and lifelong
campaigner for the environment, Jack Thomson,
from whom I and many others
have learnt much.

ACKNOWLEDGEMENTS

This book would not have been possible without the generous contribution of both the stories and personal photographs of the many men and women who relived personal and community histories.

Nor would it have been possible without the support of ABC Radio in the early 1980s, when the programmes which form the basis of this book were made. Although working very much on my own at that stage I was encouraged to develop the history radio documentary, support which led to the formation of the national Social History Unit in 1985.

In addition I must thank the following for their support and encouragement: historians Geoffrey Bolton of the University of Queensland and Hank Nelson of the Australian National University. Both read early drafts and made helpful observations. Ronda Jameson and Heather Campbell of the J S Battye Library of West Australian History were also unfailingly helpful with information and retrieval of tape transcriptions.

As the book progressed, editor Ray Coffey lent patient and supportive guidance, and Helen Garwood has, I believe, matched the mood of the oral history narrative with her careful search for the right picture.

I'd also like to acknowledge the life example provided by former forester Jack Thomson, to whom this book is dedicated. His respect for the natural environment has always inspired me, while his gift for narrative provided the title for the book.

Finally my thanks to my wife, partner and good friend, Jenny, who put up with much distraction as I began work on *Reading*

Labels on Jam Tins. We agreed on a computer curfew after a few months of writing. I am also indebted to her for perceptive proofreading and constructive criticism throughout the project.

Helen Garwood would like to thank the following people for their help with finding the illustrations for this publication: Peggy Adams; Richard Beilby; Philip Blond; Dorothy and George Brenton; Jenny Carter, Librarian, Aboriginal Affairs Planning Authority; Doug Elford, West Australian Museum; Mort and Marg Ewing; Joan and Cyril Fletcher; Sr Eileen Heath; Norma King; Sheila Laver and the late Elizabeth Laver; Margaret Morgan; Dick Mumford; Joan Pascoe; Dick Perry; Keith Quartermaine, Eastern Goldfields Historical Society; Bob Reece; Joanna Sassoon, Pictorial Collection, Battye Library; Diana Stockdale; and Doris Strang.

CONTENTS

Foreword by Geoffrey Bolton	13
Introduction	15
1. WITH DOLLYPOT, PICK AND SHOVEL Early Days on the Goldfields	23
2. ANYBODY COULD AFFORD US Aboriginal Perspectives on Twentieth-Century Australia	47
3. THEY SAID YOU'D OWN YOUR OWN FARM Group Settlement in the 1920s	75
4. A BAD BLUE The Australia Day Weekend Riots of 1934	101
5. STONYBROKE AND WALKING Memories of the Great Depression	129
6. OUT OF SIGHT, OUT OF MIND Aboriginal Internment	157
7. SOMETHING UNIQUE, SOMETHING MAJESTIC Life in the Forests	187
Pictorial References	214

FOREWORD

Australian historical writing reflects our democratic temper. In 1988 a four-volume history was produced under the name of *A People's History of Australia* taking as its main themes 'the experience of everyday life' and setting itself up as an alternative to the kind of 'history which concerns itself with the actions of well-heeled, white, Anglo-Saxon males'. But in fact a very substantial amount of Australian historical writing, perhaps a greater proportion than that of any other Western nation, is concerned with 'history from below'.

In raising our awareness of the past as reflected in the experiences of ordinary Australians — working-class men and women, migrants, ethnic minorities, spokespeople for unpopular causes — the oral historians have been well to the fore.

During the last twenty years, and especially since the founding of the Oral History Association of Australia in 1979, much has been done to recapture accounts of the past from people who might not have been in the habit of writing letters or preserving documentation. There are still a few alive who remember the 1914–18 war, more who went through the tribulations of the 1930s Depression, and a considerable number who can speak of the migrant experience on either side of the Second World War. The harvest is plentiful, and fortunately there are many experienced and able oral historians in our community who have made it their business to capture these testimonies. In so doing they have extended Australian history beyond the universities and the established historical societies. The compilation of history becomes in itself a democratic activity.

Among these oral historians Bill Bunbury commands a large measure of respect and goodwill. Through his work on Radio National, and through the ABC's local programmes in Western Australia, he has done much to increase the awareness of the wider public about the potential of oral history, and several of his ABC programmes have won a national reputation as moving and eloquent statements; one thinks particularly of his interviews with the Italian internees of the 1939–45 war period.

The present collection is focussed on various Australian themes, covering the first half of this century. Like much good oral history, this collection affords a hearing to voices sometimes unheard: the Aborigines, the rural battlers, the pick-and-shovel men and the housewives.

Bill Bunbury's two qualities of balance and compassion ensure that what we read and hear is not merely 'victim history', dwelling on oppression. His interviewees also show admirable qualities of resilience and initiative; capacity not to be beaten by adversity, but to make something of their lives. His connecting comment, humane and discerning, ensures that these episodes are as much pleasure to read as to listen to. This will be a rewarding book to own.

Geoffrey Bolton

INTRODUCTION

The sharp spring light was falling at all the right angles for filming, catching the ochre-gold of the karri trees on the northern slope, lighting up the lemon-green pasture and beginning to fade the intense blue of the Southern Ocean.

It had been a good day's shoot but I didn't know it would be one of the last documentaries I would make for ABC Television.

It was November in 1981 and we'd been filming in the Albany region, catching a little of its history, ecology and patterns of settlement.

Two months earlier I'd called into the Albany office of the Department of Agriculture.

> 'Any farmers in the Denmark area who'd mind us filming on their property? I'm looking for a good example of a mixed farm.'
> 'George Brenton'd be your man. Runs a nice place. Been there a fair while. Helpful feller. Try him!'

George was more than helpful. By the time I came back to film, he'd arranged his day so that we could film every activity and go home the next day. As the film crew said, 'If you ever give up farming George, apply to us as a production manager'.

He was changing hats every half hour, sometimes literally, shearing sheep for the camera, irrigating his potatoes, checking his fences and his steers and, towards the end of a long day, making hay while the sun still shone.

We weren't allowed to stay at the local motel.

> *Have your tea with us and shake down for the night here! Plenty of room. Save you coming back for the milking in the morning!*

Over tea I talked to Dorothy Brenton and enthused about the Denmark landscape.

'Nice country all right', Dorothy affirmed, 'George calls it "God's own"!'

It was hard to disagree. Denmark stays green most of the year, the cattle are sleek and well-fed, grazing on gentle slopes crowned by the majestic karri trees, pleasant, well-watered country. But as Dorothy said,

> *Mind you, it hasn't always looked the way it does today. What my parents would have given to see it now. They were Groupies you know! So were George's. My folk came from Scotland and George's from Devon. We all came out on this scheme as kids.*

I tried to look knowledgeable.

Moments later Dorothy produced a battered suitcase and resolved my ignorance. The case probably came out from Britain too, but its contents told an unexpected story.

Faded photos of the 1920s passed round the table; gaunt cattle grazing in half-cleared pasture, young men in double-breasted city suits and waistcoats, armed with large axes, posed self-consciously beneath enormous trees. More snaps of those same trees, prone and burnt in windrows, or, still standing, ringbarked and dead.

In contrast, cheerful kids dressed in a variety of hand-me-downs and their much more serious parents. But as George recollected,

> *Of course it was fine for us kids, we had no end of fun in the bush. It was just a big adventure for us. But our parents, well, that was a different story!*

Dorothy explained.

> *See they had no idea what they were coming to! They'd read these advertisements in the papers in England about how you could come out here, work hard for a few years and have a nice little farm to yourself in sunny Australia. None of them had any notion about the conditions here!*

As I settled to sleep that night, the Brentons' stories about the Groupies, the Group Settlers of the 1920s, their sad and faded photos, crisscrossed with the bright imagery of the farm scenes we had shot that day, like a badly edited film. It was difficult to reconcile the trim prosperity of the Brenton farm with the haunting images of their parents' struggle to clear and settle the land sixty years earlier.

Next morning, we were up and camera-ready at five, but George and Dorothy were already at work in the dairy.

Their sturdy partnership of forty years made milking look easy.

A few more landscape shots and we had finished, ready to head back to Perth.

But before we left I reminded George of our conversation over tea the previous evening. An idea was beginning to take vague shape.

> *I suppose there'd be others besides you two who'd remember the Group Settlement days.*

George scratched his head.

> *If you want, Bill, I could put you in touch with a few. There's still some of the old'uns around. There's Mrs Whitfield. She's close on a hundred now but she can still remember the old days. Then there's the Cross sisters! They*

went to the one-teacher school here. And what about Alf Tindale? He came out as a kid when we did. Oh, yes, there's a few still around.

I kept thinking about the Groupies as we drove back to Perth.

The stories the Brentons had told me were more than just interesting bits of local history, though they certainly were that too. They were part of the whole Australian story itself, the story of strangers in a strange place discovering, as every migrant generation had before them, the realities of bush life; rich, comic, heartbreaking and highly individual tales, stories that ought to be recorded, somehow.

What about a television series? The stories had dramatic potential. It was worth thinking about.

I got nowhere. There was no budget for such a venture. But I wasn't altogether sorry. All along I had felt instinctively that television wasn't the best medium for this kind of material. In any case I was busy. I had another film to make, and another.

Two years went by, but the Group Settlement story stayed in my mind like a tune I badly wanted to remember. One morning I had some time on my hands. I rang up George Brenton.

All right if I come down and start talking to some of the Groupies? I'd welcome some introductions.

Two weeks later I was back in Denmark. I had no programme budget, just a tape-recorder and a box of tapes. But the real programme resources lay ahead of me in that countryside, in the people themselves and their vivid recollections.

In July 1983 'They Said You'd Own Your Own Farm' was broadcast, first in Western Australia, and later, nationally.

The listener response was ample reward for the effort. People wrote or telephoned in with similar stories about their own experiences of life in the bush. And they told me how much they enjoyed hearing a bit of history told by ordinary people like themselves.

I made a decision. As soon as possible, I would leave television production to concentrate on radio. The medium seemed to be ideal for presenting our rich oral history. There were so many other stories to treat and, given that both our century and our people were getting older, there was a limit to the time left to capture their memories.

And that's what this book is also about: the experiences of people in a landscape, whether as migrants coping with a new culture and a new environment, or the Aboriginal experience of struggling to retain a culture and survive in a white-dominated continent. It is a social history of living through difficult times, often with fortitude, and almost invariably with humour. It is also a celebration of values and ways of life that were held dear by the people who shared them.

I am only too aware, in reproducing the original spoken word in print, of how much is lost in the process; subtle expressions of humour, compassion, courage and sadness, so evident from the tone of the human voice, but rendered more neutral by the printed page. Nonetheless, I have tried to recapture the original mood and feeling of the speakers wherever possible, aided by Helen Garwood's selection of photographs and graphic texts. And there are always the original radio programmes themselves, preserved on tape, I hope, for as long as these printed words.

All the material is re-presented as closely as possible to the spirit in which the contributors offered material to the radio programmes.

This book is the story of people whom I feel lucky to have known, and who so willingly shared with other Australians their remarkable personal histories.

And the title? *Reading Labels on Jam Tins.*

Let's just say that I hope it suggests some of the images of coping with isolation and hardship, and also something of that understated irony which helped many in difficult times. Its source, like many of the names of the chapters, lies buried in the text. I hope there are rewards for the finders.

Bill Bunbury

ABC Social History Unit
Radio National Perth
1992

READING LABELS ON JAM TINS

Seeking alluvial gold.

WITH DOLLYPOT, PICK AND SHOVEL
Early Days on the Goldfields

Well, you made do with whatever you could find – the prospectors of those days – it was a dollypot, pick and shovel and a great deal of hard work.

    Charles Barton-Jones, pioneer prospector.

Before 1892 Coolgardie and Kalgoorlie were names known only to the Wongai people who had hunted amongst the region's gimlet gums and sandalwood, conserved its sparse waterholes, and known its searing summer heat and intense night cold for tens of thousands of years.

Their quiet tenure came to a rough end in 1892 when Bayley and Ford discovered surface gold some one hundred and sixty kilometres east of Southern Cross. The find was prodigious.

Just twenty years earlier in 1872, the English novelist Anthony Trollope had visited the Swan River Colony, landing at Albany and making a four-day journey along a rough bush track to a mosquito-plagued hotel room in Perth. He was not impressed: 'I doubt if the place will prosper unless gold or other minerals be found'.

Until Arthur Bayley and John Ford's momentous find, the colony had struggled along. It was short of materials, lacked a highly viable agriculture and offered few incentives for would-be migrants. The slowness of travel and communications had kept the western third of Australia isolated from much of the political and commercial development of the eastern seaboard.

The discovery of gold brought prospectors from all over the world. But most were 't'othersiders', men from earlier gold rushes in other Australian colonies.

I spent two weeks in the Eastern Goldfields of Western Australia in 1983, finding faint traces of ghost towns like Kanowna and Larkinville, and catching some of the remaining memories of the old times in two towns that have survived, Coolgardie and Kalgoorlie. Harry Ware, former prospector:

> *Dad came over here in 1898 and on to the goldfields shortly after he came to Western Australia. I think he was sickened of land conditions in the eastern states and wanted to do something different. So he came to Western Australia because that's where everybody was coming to make their fortune.*

Dr Charles William Laver with Wongai people, late 1890s.

In 1892 thousands pushed their way into the unmapped country east of Southern Cross to try their luck on the fields. The railway line terminated at York, on the eastern edge of the Darling Ranges and only a hundred kilometres inland from Perth.

From this virtual outpost, would-be miners had to walk the best part of six hundred kilometres to the diggings. Within four years the railway line would follow their tracks to Coolgardie.

As men stocked up with provisions and equipment before heading off into the bush, the first beneficiaries of the outbreak of gold fever were the coastal ports of Fremantle and Albany, and the capital, Perth. Most prospectors walked, carrying their gear on their backs, a few rode horses, some bicycles, and one or two gave literal meaning to the expression 'pushing your own barrow'.

But their biggest concern, if they made it to the fields, and not everyone did, was water, or rather lack of it.

The further east the fewer the rivers in Western Australia, and beyond Southern Cross there are none. The country is not, as sometimes stated, desert. It is lightly forested, with plants superbly adapted to a low-rainfall environment; trees and shrubs that do not need a watercourse to cling to. But water is scarce. The lakes, where they occur at all, are mostly salt, and the only sources of fresh water are seasonal pools, filling cavities in the rock formations which break through the scrub in places.

These scarce water resources were mapped and husbanded carefully by their traditional owners, the Wongai, and were quite sufficient for their conservative lifestyle. But a procession of Europeans through their country, with horses and camels, could suck many waterholes dry in a day.

Water was to prove both a saviour and a killer in the Goldfields. Keith Quartermaine, of the Western Australian School of Mines in Kalgoorlie, described how the early diggers coped.

> *The granite rocks around here used to collect rainwater and the hollows in the rock would retain the water in gnamma hole [Aboriginal reservoir] type of formation or just plain*

'Return from Mt Ragged Rush, 1000 mile trip in the bush', c1895.

depressions. And some of the run-off from the depressions would form soaks at the bottom of the rock. And if they picked their time of year, say, following rains, they could travel quite extensively. Well, when they started stopping in places for extensive periods, that didn't work too well. And as the numbers built up they then had to devise equipment to condense the salt water in the lakes. It was rather a costly way of doing it, but it was that or perish.

The method was also costly for the environment. The price would be paid later by the future householders of Kalgoorlie and Boulder, as they swept dust from their doors, floors and windows. The only way to condense the salt water was to erect galvanised iron boilers in the bush and pass the salt water through them. The condensers were fuelled by the plentiful bush timber. That plenty was soon exploited.

So many trees were cut down for the condensers, and later to provide water for the deep underground mines at Kalgoorlie, that the miners created a dust bowl and dust storms which persisted for years after cutting had stopped.

But if miners in the larger settlements could keep going with condenser water, others, in those early years, risked contracting typhoid from polluted water. Vera Whittington, in her comprehensive account of the Western Australian gold rush, points out that typhoid had already become a severe problem in the poor sanitary conditions of late nineteenth-century Australian cities.

Perth's open drains of the 1890s were the starting point for the germ that would travel east with many young hopefuls on their way to Coolgardie. Going to the Goldfields simply worsened a digger's chance of survival.

A young physician, Doctor Charles Laver, took ship from Melbourne in 1896, landing in Albany and travelling by Cobb & Co. coach to Coolgardie. He arrived at the height of the typhoid epidemic. That experience became family history for his daughters, Elizabeth and Sheila.

Staff, Coolgardie Hospital, 1896.

> He worked in tents and of course it was very difficult. I mean hundreds of them had to die with typhoid. They didn't have the fresh fruit and vegetables of today. I don't know how they managed. You see they couldn't grow any.

Charles Laver himself survived the typhoid and travelled huge distances north of the existing diggings, riding a bicycle through unmapped bush to where the town of Laverton, named after him, now stands.

Doctors who worked on the Goldfields could only urge potential victims to ensure that they took the right vitamins. But in waterless country that was easier said than done. Doctor Daly Smith found that some of the miners developed their own ingenious solutions to the problem.

> Some would take out wheat, spread it on a wet bag, keep the bag wet and eat a handful of germinating wheat a day, and with potatoes and with whatever else they had to keep them going.

The danger, for men with gold fever, hungrier for fortune than survival, was to ignore the symptoms of the other fever. That's how author Vera Whittington saw it.

> When they were on gold they wouldn't go! They wouldn't leave it. It was a great drive. Gold was a terrific magnet.

In an incident reminiscent of Geoffrey Chaucer's Canterbury Tale of 'The Three Riotours', but perhaps with a different moral, three men in one isolated bush camp went down with typhoid. One died there, the second on the way to get help for his mates and the third cut his own throat in the last delirious stage of his illness.

If you visit the cemetery at 'The Old Camp' (Coolgardie) today you can read, on many gravestones, the fate of those who came for

'Water sold here 4d', Goldfields water supply, 1895.

gold and met an early death instead. Almost one in five who caught typhoid died of it. And the epidemic put enormous strain on the already stretched medical resources of the State. Even before the gold rush there was a shortage of hospitals, medical equipment and nurses, a situation that was only relieved by the courageous efforts of both bush nurses and sisters from religious orders. These women worked from hastily improvised tent hospitals, often with little or no clean water and limited medical supplies. Without their efforts many more would have perished. As it was, these nurses were still unable to reach those who died out in the bush, as often from thirst as from typhoid.

Water, or its scarcity, was the chief preoccupation for the mushroom towns which sprouted in the wake of the first gold scramble. For Cecile Shelley's family in Kalgoorlie (she was later to campaign as a trade union official for better working conditions for women), water was always short.

> *You see the water was coming from the mines, and there was, I suppose, a rush on it. And Mum kept a goat, you see, so we could always get milk. And one day when we had no water she had to buy lemonade and give the goat a drink. I'll never forget that! I thought it was a terrible thing to go and give a goat lemonade when I could have drunk it. And I can still see that goat with the sniffles of lemonade round its nose as the poor thing was having a drink that Mum had to buy for it. We had to buy the water too! We had to pay two and six for a kerosene tin of water. You had to be very scarce with it. And we had to have fewer baths or more of us had to bath in the same water, which we didn't like. We used to quarrel over who'd be first, who'd be second, who'd be third and fourth.*

Western Australia had been unprepared for the rapid growth in population (numbers trebled inside ten years) and the consequent demand for services in the first years of the gold rush. But, suddenly conscious of the wealth gold brought into the

Building the pipeline for the Goldfields water supply, c1902.

colony, the government made rapid amends.

What was and remains one of Australia's most ambitious engineering projects, the Goldfields Water Scheme, brought fresh water to the Goldfields in 1903.

Masterminded by the State's Chief Engineer, C Y O'Connor, a pipeline slowly crawled up from the brand new Mundaring Reservoir in the Darling Ranges and across the plateau, still climbing to Kalgoorlie, almost four hundred metres above sea level, pushed on its way by wood-fired pumping stations right across the Wheatbelt. As Cecile Shelley observed, the effect on the dusty Kalgoorlie townsite was immediate.

> *Oh, it was marvellous, you know. Gardens sprang up all round the Goldfields, with the water coming from Perth.*

But the water wasn't pushed all that way just to nourish gardens. Huge quantities were needed for large-scale gold extraction from deep underground mines. By 1901 the gold-mining scene was radically different from the early days in nearby Coolgardie. Prospector Paddy Hannan had discovered 'The Mile That Midas Touched', at Kalgoorlie, forty kilometres east of Coolgardie, and further excavation revealed the presence of huge gold seams at a considerable depth below the surface. For prospectors like Paddy Hannan, who did not retire rich, the era of alluvial mining and the days of fossicking in the bush and moving on were almost over. Occasionally an individual prospector working on an isolated claim could still strike it lucky, but for the most part the wealth now lay well underground.

So big capital and big companies moved in and the small men went to work for wages or moved out. Many of the original miners left to try their luck elsewhere. The life of wage slavery was not for them. They were explorers as much as prospectors, men who lived for the open air and the freedom as much as for the dream of striking el dorado.

Their spirit and lifestyle still survive today in the part-time prospectors, often retired city dwellers, who swap the ennui of the suburb for the solitude of the bush, trying their luck on their own for a few weeks every year far out in the bush

Some prospectors, if they had struck it lucky, bought a farm nearer the coast or a shop in the city. Others were replaced by migrants from Italy and the Adriatic coast, men who had heard about the gold in Western Australia but arrived to find it locked up in the big new mines. But that was still where the work was.

So they trickled up from Fremantle and into the Goldfields where they became, for a time, part of the new industrial population of the gold industry. Slavs, in particular, worked on the woodline, cutting timber for the pit props.

Most settled in Kalgoorlie or nearby Boulder. Some immigrants settled for jobs labouring underground. Their entry into the workforce was to give rise to tensions immediately after World War One and during the Great Depression. More of that in a subsequent chapter.

By 1903 Coolgardie, which had started as a row of tents in 1892, was already known as 'The Old Camp'. For ten years it had been the end of the railway line, running up from Perth six hundred kilometres to the west. Retired mining registrar Rex Mitchell knew that pre-war Coolgardie well.

> *I can recollect camel teams in Coolgardie, horse and donkey teams as well. There were no motor cars, not until about 1908–1910. The first car was bought by the newsagent. The rest of us used to walk or bike. If you owned a bike you were in the upper bracket.*

Coolgardie would not remain at the end of the line for much longer as the railway pushed still further east to the new camp – Kalgoorlie. Norma King, a Goldfields author and historian, knows both communities well.

> *There was a lot of jealousy between the two towns. This brash Kalgoorlie was starting to take over. By about 1897 there was a*

> tremendous building activity in Kalgoorlie. The Palace Hotel was built and that was something really very special. They scoured Europe for its beautiful furnishings.

Not long after Federation Kalgoorlie could boast tram services in its main streets, and railway lines linked the outlying Goldfields towns to each other and to Perth. It was now a town where married couples came to earn a living. Men still outnumbered women two to one but the balance was shifting. Norma King whose book, *Daughters Of Midas*, portrays the lives of Goldfields women, relates that her own grandmother

> came over here in 1897, following her husband and it was extremely hard for her. It was hard for all women. I mean the lack of water here. See, we didn't get our pipeline until 1903, so everything had to be condensed or caught in rainwater, so it was always the problem all the time. And I remember she had a very unfortunate experience, because her husband was killed as she was coming over from Adelaide. Fortunately, she had a sister here who helped her. But she lived in a hessian hut and there was no window, just a slit in the wall and a stick to prop it open.
>
> And life was extremely hard for her because there was no breadwinner. And she had six children, with only one capable of earning. All she could do to keep her family going, because there were no pensions then, was to take in washing. Washing and ironing. And of course that meant hand-scrubbing, with a tub and a copper. Really hard work.

For the male migrants who were finding their way to the Goldfields, only a few years later, life and work were also still hard. When Joe Zekulich arrived in Fremantle from Dalmatia in 1916, he was advised by the fellow countrymen who gathered to meet him off the ship that there was little work in Perth. He'd be better off trying his luck on the mines at Kalgoorlie. This advice was fre-

Prospector's camp, Kalgoorlie, c1935.

quently given to young immigrants, and many of those who took it did so at the cost of their lives.

Joe Zekulich didn't go underground but he saw many who did.

> *For three months I'd been on a mine looking for a job, watching those men coming from the lift or skip, whatever they call it. You couldn't see anything of them except their eyes and teeth. All the rest was covered with the dust, just as if you splashed cement all over their clothes and all that. And when they coughed you could hear them a long way off. And when they bring up their spit it was terrible, just as if you got mixed cement from their lungs. And very few of those men are left to live a full life. They all die young and when I visited Kalgoorlie on a couple of occasions, later, I saw men that I knew. When you see them on the street, it would break your heart to see how they looked, nothing but bone and skin. And they're all yellow and coughing terribly.*

Joe Zekulich's comments are echoed by Lorenzo Mazza, who also decided to fossick on the surface rather than go underground.

> *You couldn't see each other for the dust. They used to bore into quartz. Well, if you bore into quartz, you swallowed a certain amount of quartz with the air you breathed in. It played havoc with your lungs. That's why so many died of the miner's complaint.*

But apart from the near certainty of developing silicosis or the dreaded 'dusting', a disease that often didn't show up for years, there were other everyday risks for those who worked underground. Cecile Shelley's mother was determined that 'her boys were not going down those mines because nearly every day the whistle went. Somebody got killed in the mines.'

Risks abounded. Shafts could collapse through flimsy propping or flood suddenly after a thunderstorm. Today, in a more health

Miners' camp, Goldfields, c1890.

and safety-conscious climate, we question why such conditions were allowed to prevail. Two answers stand out.

There were few alternatives to employment in the mines. The Western Australian economy in those inter-war years offered little else to wage earners. And there was always the prospect of bringing more out of the mine than wages. Taking sly gold home in your boots or under your hat was a common practice, so common that the police set up special gold squads to catch the offenders. Mavis Hodgetts of Kalgoorlie knew one or two who got away.

> *So many men made their fortunes through taking the gold from the mine. Some of them would plant it and then go back later on at night for it. I remember one man who made a lot of money here. He hid it in his mouth! There's many miners left here wealthy men and went elsewhere. That's how they made their money then.*

Tom Ryan tells a gold-stealing yarn that has now passed into Goldfields folklore.

> *There was this fellow, Paddy. And the police really had it in for him. So one night two constables came over and searched his place from top to bottom in front of Paddy's terrified wife, Mary. And while the detectives were going through every drawer and cupboard, Paddy came home from the pit, still wearing his mining clothes. And he sat down at the kitchen table and put his feet up, enjoying the sight of the police officers sweating away and finding nothing. And being a cheeky sort, he asked them if they'd mind pulling his boots off while they were about it. They swore at him and kept on rummaging through drawers and cupboards. But soon afterwards they gave up and went, slamming the door behind them. Mary immediately rounded on her husband. 'Why did you provoke them so?' Paddy slid his boots off the table and began to undo the laces. 'And where do you think I was keeping the bloody gold?'*

Other gold smugglers, equally astute, took their ill-gotten gains interstate, via the Trans-Australian train across the Nullarbor. Whenever they got a tip-off, gold squad detectives searched the interstate trains from end to end before they left Kalgoorlie. But they didn't think to look inside the ever-simmering stove in the guard's van at the back of the train. Not hot enough to melt lumps of gold but warm enough in the hide-and-seek game of gold stealing.

Unfortunately, there was a more violent side to gold stealing, culminating in the deaths of police detectives Pitman and Walsh in 1926, murdered as they apprehended a gold-stealing gang. This episode has been accurately and dramatically depicted in the ABC Television feature *Hands Of Gold*, written and produced by Tony Evans in 1976.

Paradoxically, as the Depression of the 1930s tightened its grip over Australia, Kalgoorlie regained something of its earlier rush. With the collapse of jobs in almost every sector of the economy, and the failure of the international investment market, gold was in strong demand from investors nervous of every other index of wealth. Once again men flocked from all over Australia to the Western Goldfields, as they had done in the 1890s.

This time, however, they were not coming to fossick for their fortune but to take their chance in the long queues which formed each day at the mine entrance. (Digger) Charles Daws saw, day after day,

> *upwards of a hundred men standing around the shaft head waiting to see if they could get one shift underground, if somebody didn't turn up sick. And the shift boss of those days, he'd come out and look at the crowd. And he'd pick the biggest bloke right at the back and he'd say: 'Right! You come over here. And all you other buggers, you go home.'*

But Depression or no Depression, there was still the odd lucky strike, out in the bush and away from the company mines.

On 15 January 1931, the Larcombes, father and son, were

prospecting together in the bush. They had just taken up a block abandoned by another prospector as 'no good' and, after working on it for just a few hours, unearthed the largest nugget ever found in Australia, 'The Golden Eagle'. The site was Larkinville, some seventy kilometres south of Coolgardie.

Former prospector Chris Wood was minding the nearby Larkinville store, when

> The dish rang. They had a dish which they used to ring when anything important was on. The shop was full of men but it wasn't too long before it emptied out. Pat, who was working with me, went up to have a look (it was only two or three hundred yards away). And he was soon back and said, 'Go and see! Go and see! It's bigger than a frying pan!' That was one of our sayings. They'd be unearthing something bigger than a frying pan. So I said, 'Right, I'll go and see it'. When I got there it was lying on the ground where he'd picked it out and old Mr Jim (Mr Larcombe Senior) was reading a letter he'd just received. Funny! It was to tell them they'd just stopped all his credit at the grocers.
>
> Anyway, I went across and spoke to young Jim. 'Do you mind if I try the weight?' And I picked it up and tried the weight and when I put it down everyone wanted to have a go. Anyhow they all tried it. Later we weighed it at the store and it came to over seventy pounds, over a thousand ounces. There was a little discussion while it was lying on the ground there about what it would be named.
>
> They asked the older Mr Larcombe. 'Oh, it's going to be called "Little Jim"' (after his son).
>
> 'Oh, no you can't call it that! But, by gee, it looks like a lion!'
> 'No, it's going to be called "Little Jim".'
> 'Now, you turn it round the other way, it looks like a camel!'
> And after a little while it got turned up the other way. Somebody was trying it for weight and a little old bloke with a goatee beard like Uncle Sam said: 'Look at that, Jim. It looks

The Larcombes, Jim senior and junior, with the Golden Eagle, 1931.

like an eagle! You sell it to the American government and they'll pay you anything for it!' But Mr Larcombe, he stuck to 'Little Jim'. He said: 'Anyhow how would you fellers sell it to the Yanks? Scaddan [Minister for Mines] *wouldn't let you!'* [No gold could be privately exported in 1931.] *But the name stuck, and it's appropriate because it does look like a golden eagle.*

The Larcombes did well enough with their find, valued then at the equivalent of nearly twelve thousand dollars. (At today's prices they might have been millionaires.) The family settled for town life, buying the Terminus Hotel in Kalgoorlie and renaming it 'The Golden Eagle'. The pub was probably a good investment, given the steady growth of the town in the 1930s.

And the Golden Eagle itself?

Melted down and dispersed. Many Goldfields towns and the railway lines that reached them were to share a similar fate, their steel, timber and iron buildings torn up and moved on, carted away to make other roofs and walls, in the relentless, often elusive search for other el dorados.

As prospector Howard Ware put it: 'Gold is the only thing I know very much about so I've remained on the Fields'.

But there is another lure besides gold in that dry country east of Southern Cross. For Goldfielders like Doris Bartlett it has always been home. 'There is something about the Goldfields that makes you always want to go back again.'

And for Nurse Alice Flood, 'It fascinated me. It still does. I'll be buried in the red soil up here.'

(Based on the ABC Radio documentary broadcast in June 1983)

Prospectors' camp near Kalgoorlie, c1895.

Domestic training class, Moore River Settlement.

ANYBODY COULD AFFORD US
Aboriginal Perspectives on Twentieth-Century Australia

We were servants, trained as servants, just cheap labour for middle-class white people who could afford – well, for that matter, anybody could afford us, I suppose.

Iris Clayton, poet and author.

Iris Clayton, like so many Aboriginal children in the 1930s, was taken from her family in outback New South Wales. She spent the rest of her childhood and adolescence at Cootamundra Home for Aboriginal girls.

'Anybody Could Afford Us' is based on a documentary I made in 1986. That broadcast tried to provide an Aboriginal perspective on the Australian pre-war world and the conditions that prevailed for these Australians well into the 1950s and 1960s. I am indebted to anthropologist Marcia Langton and political leader Robert Riley for the insights that form the basis of this narrative.

Iris Clayton's story is fairly typical of the pre-World War Two Aboriginal generation, with its almost inevitable components, family break-up, recruitment of cheap labour, and the struggle to survive in a dominant white culture. Her experience could be recounted from one side of the Australian continent to the other, from places as far apart as Moore River in Western Australia and Cootamundra in New South Wales, where Iris Clayton said goodbye to her family.

Well, my parents were separated. And then the welfare came out. And there were six of us taken – the eldest six. There was nine in my family altogether, but the eldest six, we were just put on a train and taken off to Cootamundra. Well the whole of Waterloo was very upset at the time. We had people crying all week before we went. And we got to Cootamundra – my mother took me there. She said, 'It's just going to be a holiday, like, it'll only be for a little while and we'll all be back together'.

But we found out, of course, rather differently that it wasn't. Matron met us down at the railway station. And then we got up to the homes. And the first thing she did was shove us all in the hot bath, and cut our hair off (we had very long hair those days) and scrubbed us until we were practically pink. And then they checked the bathtub after us to see if there was any ring around it. It was incredible really. It was a good thing my mother bathed us in the morning before we went. But that was the introduction to Cootamundra – bath and haircut.

Matron with babies, Moore River Settlement.

Iris Clayton went to Cootamundra alone. Her brothers were sent to Kinchella Boys Home. She wasn't to see them again until she was sixteen. The other children remained with their mother.

The close bonds of extended kinship are especially important to Aboriginal communities, and the sudden loss of family has always been a grievous injury to both Aboriginal children and their parents. Iris lost touch with both her grandmothers, women to whom she was very close.

> *I missed them terribly, and it was very, very hard to settle down there for a while. We did write backwards and forwards, but matron always read our mail, so if there was anything there that she didn't think should be there, she'd cross it out, like somebody died, or like whenever I heard of any deaths, or if your mother was coming to see you and she was going to get in touch with matron, well that was crossed out and matron would say, 'I've crossed that out because your mother was going to come and see you, but I don't think it's allowable at this stage'. So you weren't allowed to see your parents either. You felt cut off, really cut right off! They tried to wipe out your whole family background in the one heap. You were kept away from all relationships like that.*

The removal of children from their parents, the splitting up of families, forced removals of groups and entire families to different stations and reserves was common throughout Australia. Most of the girls taken away from their families were eventually shoved into domestic service for low wages and low expectations.

For Iris Clayton Cootamundra was simply a training environment for work in a white world.

> *You got up at half six in the morning. The first thing you did was strip your bed or the staff stripped it for you. Your bed was made under supervision. They used to bounce a sixpence on it.*

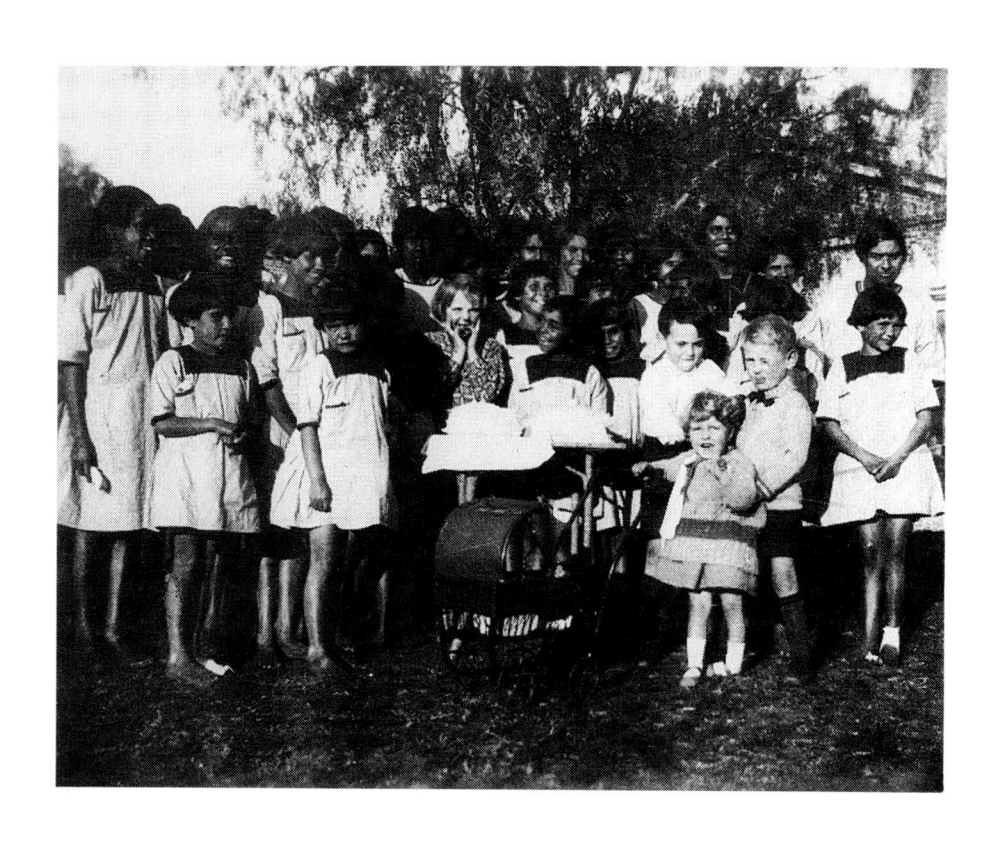

Cootamundra House, New South Wales, c1930.

> If it wasn't made properly, your bed would be stripped down again, and you'd have to remake your bed until it was done properly.

Formal education was minimal and further studies were not encouraged. Only three or four of Iris Clayton's contemporaries came away with the Intermediate Certificate.

> There was like, you know, keep them dumb and black. That was the whole idea because, you know, no white person wanted an educated blackfellow working for them, telling them what to do.

Perhaps the strongest educational force at Cootamundra was the pressure on the girls to lose their Aboriginality.

> We were sort of brought up with white outlooks. We were never taught black things, like if we used Aboriginal words at the home, we were punished, or if we sort of sp' black, we were punished. And there was a family there who had a real Aboriginal accent and matron checked them often. 'I'll have none of that black talk here!' which is a shame because they were lovely girls. They had a true, natural sort of, real, lovely flowing Aboriginal accent, and it's just taught out of them. It's a sad story really because there was suicides, there was prostitution, there was alcoholism. And a lot of girls have died from cirrhosis of the liver through being alcoholics. And a hell of a lot has committed suicide, because they just couldn't cope with being black, but not being black.

Over three thousand kilometres away, on the other side of Australia, Bella Yappo's family lived in the Eastern Goldfields of Western Australia. Bella also spent her childhood in an institution. Moore River Native Settlement, as it was called then, was a place where part-Aboriginal children were sent to be brought up as

Iris Clayton at Cootamundra, c1950.

Europeans, albeit second-class ones. In effect, Bella was penalised for having a black mother, and her mother punished for cohabiting with a white feller.

> The man that my mother was living with, he was a well sinker, and the police came out and picked us up, so she just packed up and we came in to Wiluna. We were there for a couple of days until the train was coming to Perth. So they put us on a train, and then someone else met us in Perth. We didn't know where we were going or anything – well I didn't. And we come to Mogumber [Moore River Native Settlement] by train. We were scared because everybody's staring at you and want to know where you come from. Some of them were nasty and some of them weren't. And my brothers – I didn't know where they were going or – well, I was only young. And I had two cousins go at the same time, and I was sort of out on a limb. And I just had to make the best of it. I didn't know where they were going or anything.

In the years after World War Two, Aboriginal leader Rob Riley spent his own childhood in a children's home, Sister Kate's, in Perth, and found his parents again only after a long separation. He sees broken childhoods, like those of Bella Yappo and Iris Clayton, as destructive influences in the lives of many Aboriginal people.

> I don't know whether words can explain the sense of belonging that one can have to a family that you've never known. Just having people that were your own flesh and blood, you always want to know where you come from, where your roots are. There are many people in the situation where they don't know where their families are or where they come from, so that sense of not belonging to anybody would be still even more traumatic. And I think that's impermeated in people that say, that have been adopted out, and still say later on, even twenty, thirty years later, they're saying they want to find out who their mother and father are.

As Robert Riley sees these decades, the 1920s and 1930s were a period in which governments assumed that the Aboriginal race was going to die out, and accordingly legislated to make that process more comfortable for the conscience of white society. The resulting policy of assimilation took no account of family relationships and often assumed that they did not exist. Marcia Langton blames institutions like Moore River and Cootamundra for much of the damage to individual lives.

> *I think most people are shattered by the experience, and have spent most of their adult lives trying to find their families, and trying to come to terms with being Aboriginal in this society. For those people the effect has been a deep psychological hurt.*

Iris Clayton certainly saw Cootamundra in that light.

> *Cootamundra achieved that effect. It helped me in the white society but it didn't help me with the black society. I mean you went back to your parents, but they were complete strangers. All your relations were. Everybody was just as strange to each other. As I've told you, there was nine of us taken, there were nine of us in the family, but six of us were taken. Now there's a bit of a gap between the ones that were taken to Cootamundra and the ones that were left home with Mum. There's a gap there. There's not that closeness between us. It really affected the whole family, the family structure.*

Institutions like Moore River and Cootamundra not only took children away from their own families. They also pushed them out again, but not back into their familiar surroundings. Iris Clayton awoke one morning to be told it was her last day at Cootamundra. She was hurriedly prepared for an exit into black work for white employers.

You were given a sort of book when you first went to work. Oh! That was another thing too. You left school and then you got up and matron would say to you, 'Look, you're going to work today!' You didn't know anything about it beforehand. So you rushed around. The staff packed your bags the night before. Then you had to rush around, say your goodbyes to your family, and you didn't know when the hell you were going to see them again – your sisters and brothers. That was rough – oh, that was terrible, not knowing, you know.

Anyways, you were scrubbed up and chucked in the car and halfway to Canberra, I said to matron, 'Where am I going?' And she said, 'Oh, Canberra!' That was halfway here. I was halfway here and she told me I was coming to Canberra. And then you were given this book, you see. 'Now', she said, 'this is your booklet. Those are your wages. You've got to sign that each week.' And there was two and six for me, that's twenty-five cents today. Ten shillings had to go into my bank account, and she said, 'Make sure you sign that and make sure that they pay you!' And that was the first time I'd ever handled money. I was fifteen years old and I was given two and six a week, you know, and I thought Whoopee! I'm rich. I'm going to save up and buy a house so I can get my brothers and sisters out of the home! And on ten shillings a week I had high dreams, oh yes. Of course, that didn't come about. I still don't own a house or land.

The policies which gave rise to Cootamundra and Moore River had already taken their effect on one generation of Aboriginal people. Doris Collard, of Perth, began her working life in the 1930s.

Domestic work, that's all we could do but we weren't paid that much in them days. Sometimes I thought well, things could be better for us, just working as maids and waiting on white people and that sort of thing.

Iris Clayton's first job was as a domestic servant in suburban Canberra.

> *I was all right. I was treated all right. But a lot of girls weren't. Some of the girls went out on to the stations. And they ended up being pregnant by the station owners themselves. Then those girls that were made pregnant out on these stations were sent to Sydney, to Parramatta Girls Home, for being uncontrollable. And then their kids were either adopted out or they were given abortions. And these are the ones that went into prostitution, who were servants, trained as servants, just cheap labour for middle-class white people who could afford – well, for that matter, anybody could afford us!*
>
> *You weren't taught anything about money, not a thing. We didn't even know what 'award' meant. The only award we knew, like the word 'award', would be a ward of the state, not award in wages.*

For both sexes, expectations and aspirations were equally low. Girls became domestic drudges and boys exploited pastoral workers, providing the cheap labour which underpinned whole sectors of the rural economy.

Ivan Yarran worked with his father on Wheatbelt farms in the late 1950s.

> *They talk about when the white fellow went up there and how he worked, and when he downed tools to get his farm where it is now. And that's not true at all. I remember me old man was a cutter and he used to do a lot of cutting down with an axe. And he cleared a lot of property. And when he finished clearing five or six hundred acres, whatever it was, the boss came down after he had finished. And he said, 'Well you've done a good job!' He says, 'Here's your pay!' He gave him an old shotgun and a sack of flour.*

Twenty years earlier, just before World War Two, Bella Yappo had married an agricultural worker. They went to work on a farm near Moora.

You never had a house to live in – no way. If you didn't have a tent you had to get some tins from the dump, or cut some bags and sew it together and make a tent. I just couldn't live in a tent, not in a tent and a bag hut, so I carried all this timber and – no furniture – stick bed! I carted all the sticks for our bed. We had to because the snakes were there, and put four sticks in the kitchen, got some wood from the dump, and made a table. We've never had a house to walk in to, never!

In post-war Australia, Ivan Yarran's family had a home of sorts!

We lived in a two-bedroomed camp the old man built himself. It didn't have any flooring, ground flooring and things like that. We worked for a farmer who lived in a six or eight bedroom house. He just accepted that, that we should be living in those conditions. There was no question about it. We didn't have any running water. We used to cart our water. I mean, in the winter, it was just impossible to have showers and things like that. And in the morning Mum used to go outside and make a big fire and that's how she used to cook our breakfast. If it was raining we had to try and have our breakfast in between showers without getting wet. We lived in those conditions for at least ten years.

There was a white bloke helping, because his [the farmer] was getting bigger and he employed a white bloke. He had one child and his wife and himself, and before he got there, he built him a new house. It was a three-bedroom house, but it was brand new. And that's where he went to live – we were still living in our camp. He didn't ask us if we wanted anything else. He knew how we lived and he accepted that.

Aboriginal fringe dwellers camp, late 1930s.

As Rob Riley points out, white farmers had come to depend on black labour and skill.

> The whole opening up of the rural industry, particularly the farming industry, was done with the knowledge of Aboriginal people showing the farmers, in the early days of the settlers, where the best areas of lands were and things like that.

Knowledge that, for Ivan Yarran's family, went largely unrewarded.

> We didn't get the other things that the other shearers got, like lunch and having live-in and showers and things like that. I remember one day, it was lunch time, and we knocked off for lunch. We were standing outside, and all of a sudden a guy came over with my lunch and my old man's lunch in his hand, and he says, 'You can have it here, on the woodheap if you want, but you can't eat inside!' Of course we told him that's his sheep, let him shear 'em. If we weren't good enough to eat at his table we weren't good enough to shear his sheep. Well, he went hysterical and he said, 'Ah, I didn't mean to say that. I didn't know it would affect you.' And he was talking to a human being, and when I think about it, it seems to me that he didn't know that.

Aboriginal people had to cope with being on the bottom rung of the economic and social ladder of Australian society and were also denied the social and political freedom other Australians took for granted.

Rob Riley argues that this deprivation took its toll right up to the 1950s.

> Even as recently as thirty or forty years ago, Aboriginal people were treated as aliens within their own country, and made to feel inferior.

Aboriginal camp, Mount Margaret Mission, c1948.

Playwright Jack Davis experienced those conditions both as a child and as an adult.

> *In those days, and to a lesser extent even today, the ways of living by Aboriginal people were determined by higher authorities, by the government of the day, and certainly by Native Welfare.*
>
> *We couldn't do anything unless it was with the express approval of those sorts of parties. We knew we couldn't really go into town all that often without feeling guilty, and that the police had total and sole authority over our lives in regards to where we were and what we were doing.*
>
> *The whole world screams about laws – apartheid in South Africa. But we had those laws long before South Africa did, in Australia, to keep Aboriginal people down. It wasn't set up to keep Aboriginal people down. It was set up because they believed in the 'dying pillow' policy. They thought Aboriginal people were dying out. Well, they were dying out back in the 1870s and the 1880s and the 1890s, but they didn't realise that the Aboriginal population was growing, especially the part-Aboriginal population, and these 'dying pillow' policies were still carried out, such as laws where you had to leave the town at six o'clock. That was put in for your own protection. But those laws were still in existence in the thirties when they no longer applied, but nobody worried about changing them. So those laws to us were oppression. If you were told to get home at six o'clock, if you didn't do it, well, you were slammed in gaol.*

Nyungar elder and teacher the late Ned Mippey lived in the shadow of the curfew, working between the wars in country towns in the Midland district of Western Australia.

> *There was places where you were told, 'Out at Six! Out at six! Get your tucker by six now', and if he [the local policeman] caught you there, he'd rough you, rough you up. Perhaps throw you in. I know because I ran with the others. I kept saying you*

> know, 'Out! Come on! Get your tucker and get!' Well, see we didn't have any of this legal aid. We had nothing, nothing, and if they said, 'Shift!', you shifted.

In country towns and also around the capital, Perth, Aborigines were forced to live on the edges of town as fringe dwellers. Many stayed that way. It was a lifestyle that Ned Mippey's family knew only too well.

> *I put myself down as a scrounger! All I lived on was selling bottles, scrap metal and anything I could sell – prop sticks [for clothes lines], cobweb brooms, we used to make them for the ladies. The main things there was there then was props, selling prop sticks and, mind you, that was hard! Me Dad used to carry six forked sticks and I'd only carry two! I'd get rid of mine and he'd say, 'Oh, well! Take some tucker home to Mum.'*

Political activist Bob Bropho's Perth childhood was spent

> *living under wheatbags. And I remember my father cutting the sticks of the peppermint tree to make a shade and making stick beds, and putting peppertree leaves down for mattresses, and continuously going out and walking the streets, asking people for old clothes and selling cool drink bottles, and asking for stale bread and things like that. That's a fringe-dwelling lifestyle of Aboriginal people in the thirties, mid-thirties, coming right away up till now.*

Aboriginal poverty, like white poverty, was exacerbated by the conditions of the Depression. But towards the end of the 1930s, with the threat of war in both Europe and Asia, the armed forces offered the best chance for employment in a decade. When Aboriginal men put on the khaki, they were aspiring to paid work and, equally important, seeking recognition within Australian society. Marcia Langton, however, sees this period as offering false hope.

The history of the Second World War in the Torres Straits, or in north Queensland, or New South Wales, is quite different. In New South Wales, for instance, the Aboriginal leadership went to fight for Australia, believing that that would be a step to citizenship. How disappointed they were!

Rob Riley agrees.

I mean just imagine how traumatic it must have been for returned servicemen who'd gone away and fought with the risk of their life, to come back to a country and having to fall into the requirements of getting an Act so that they could walk the street that they had so valiantly gone overseas to defend. I mean the very fact that Aboriginal people even involved themselves in the war effort, Aboriginal people enlisted in the armed forces, went across overseas, some died for the cause in that respect.

That's something that's not recognised as such, as being one of the positive contributions that Aboriginal people have made to this country. I've known of many, many instances where returned Aboriginal servicemen came back to this country, after fighting for the country, and not being accepted as equals, and in that respect, Aboriginal people weren't afforded the same opportunities in relation to farm allotments that a lot of returned servicemen were entitled to.

Returned soldier Jim Brennan had gone to World War Two from the Eastern Goldfields of Western Australia.

When I got discharged out of the army, we went up to Leonora. All our friends were up there. I couldn't walk in with them to have a drink, you know. You couldn't get a decent house to live in. Even the police was checking on you whether after six o'clock at night, if you get caught in the street, he run you in, you

Jimmy Brennan (left) with Doris and Bert Thomas, Mount Margaret Mission, 1945.

> understand. I ended up fighting against it. I said, 'I went away and fought for me country'. I said, 'Why should I come back as a migrant, you know? I was bred and born here.'

Unlike Jim Brennan, John Collard received limited recognition for his wartime service. His son, Dean Collard, describes the family's lifestyle in the South-west in the mid-1940s.

> Dad was a returned soldier. He was allocated a block of land, twelve acres, and a house that had no electricity, no running water or anything. There was a well that was dug by my parents. There was a soak at the other end of the paddock from which we had to draw water and, in fact, that was one of our duties. We had a bucket and us kids used to go up the other end of the paddock and draw the water and lump it back to the house. In fact I remember, the only baths we did have was every Sunday because of that difficulty.

Dean grew up and went to school from that country home. In 1955 school wasn't compulsory for Aboriginal children.

> It was a difficult experience for most of us Aboriginal kids. We weren't allowed to live inside the town limits, and that's the reason why that reserve was two miles outside of town. We were virtually betwixt and between I guess. You had farm children going to school; and they had transport, they had school buses; and you had town children living within the township going to the school; and you had us, the Aboriginal children, walking to school often without proper school uniform, nine times out of ten without any shoes on your feet etc. – tramping the couple of miles to school, and then fronting up to the teachers, sometimes late, sometimes without breakfast. All those sorts of problems which often was difficult for teachers and other, non-Aboriginal school children to understand.

School children, Moore River Settlement, 1949.

Even friendships across the boundaries of race and culture could hold out false promise.

> I can remember one incident at school where one of my best friends, in fact, was a non-Aboriginal fellow. He was a farmer's son and his father was quite rich, but he did invite me out to his house on a weekend and I then immediately thought of things like toothpaste and toothbrushes which I didn't have. I didn't have those things. No Aboriginal kid did, underpants and singlets and so on. So I went home with that request to my Mum to – and Dad – to see if they could get those things together with a small case. I mean we got all those things together and on the Friday when I took the case to school, this best friend of mine then told me that I couldn't go out there because his sister, who was a model in the city, was coming back and he had told his parents and sister about me coming out there, an Aboriginal kid.
>
> I knew my friend very well, and I knew that he had problems with explaining that to his parents and so on, and they couldn't accept that an Aboriginal person was going to go out there on the farm. I mean that really made me feel low. I didn't ever get out there to see him or his farm.

For Ivan Yarran, who also grew up in the country, school itself was something to be endured.

> We used to cop the cane, I guess, three or four times as much as any ordinary white European would, and when we came to school, we came to school as a disadvantaged people. We never had the kind of things it was our right to have. We weren't dressed like the ordinary schoolkids was. I remember going to school without even any pair of shoes. I used to have a pair of football boots, and that's all I had, and I wasn't allowed to wear them inside because they would scrape the floor, they told me, the sprigs on the boots. So I used to never wear them except every Friday, and every other day I used to go to school with no shoes

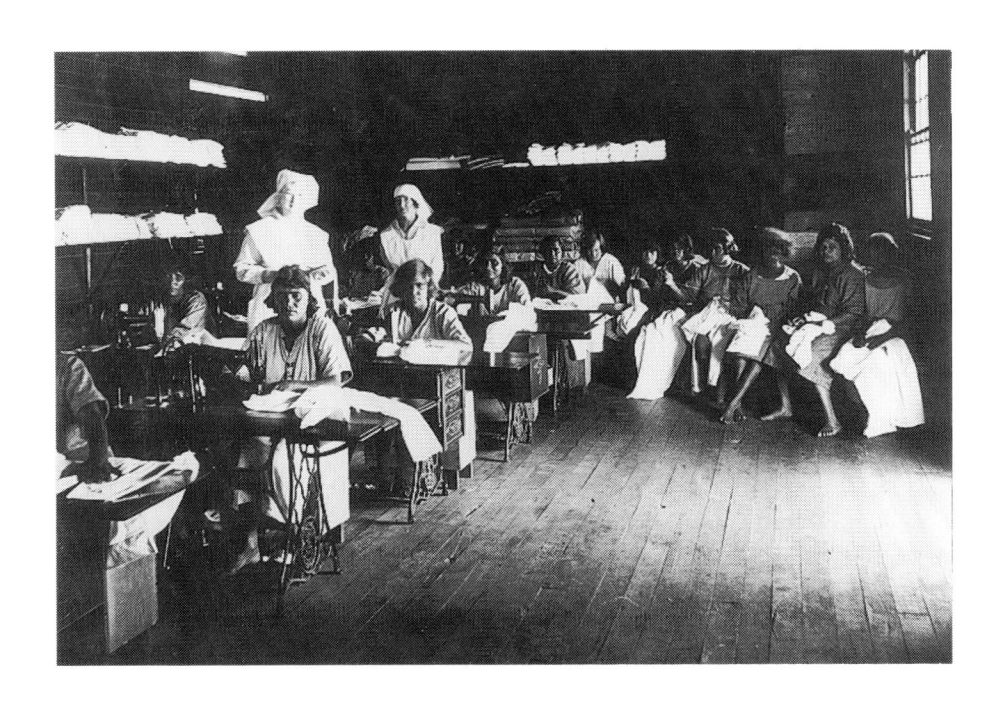

Sewing room, Moore River Settlement, 1925.

> on, because we couldn't afford another pair of shoes for myself.
>
> And I used to have to try and sit down and study, and my feet were cold, and I was thinking about what I'm going to have for lunch and things like that. Those are the disadvantages, I think, the average Aboriginal people would have experienced.

And for Dean Collard even the school curriculum could estrange him from the rest of the class.

> The history that we were taught was history about English history. The curriculum for all children, including Aboriginal, was that it taught about English history and the early days of colonisation. I mean the only reference to Aboriginal history was the fact that they were Aboriginal and they were savages and they had spears and hunted kangaroos. It often reinforced these ideas along with the fact that we had to live outside of town and all those other things, like not having the correct uniform – that we were second-class citizens, and the fact that the history books made reference to 'savages' and that we carried spears and that we killed white settlers again reinforced the feeling that we were inferior.

Rob Riley emphasises that it is essential, however difficult, for Europeans to come to terms with the Aboriginal experience.

> The fact that Aboriginal people now themselves are involved in attempting to address the many issues, and the experiences of Aboriginal people, is something that no European, no matter how involved or how committed they are to Aboriginal issues, will never ever have the understanding or the appreciation, simply because they've never had the experience of being an Aboriginal in Australia.

And a final word from Marcia Langton.

Kindergarten, Moore River Settlement, 1936.

We've been here since time immemorial and we want our children to understand what it means to be Aboriginal, and that is, that our children must know who they are.

(Based on the ABC Radio documentary broadcast in June 1983)

Charity, 1934.

Group Settlement homestead, Northcliffe, 1925.

THEY SAID YOU'D OWN YOUR OWN FARM
Group Settlement in the 1920s

And they said that within five years you would own your own farm. Well, naturally, we didn't expect to see miles and miles of trees, did we?

Florence Trudgeon, Group Settler.

In Western Australia Group Settlement was the brainchild of Sir James Mitchell, who became State Premier in 1919. Coming, as he did, from a successful farming family in the long-settled and fertile Avon valley, Mitchell could see no reason why a land settlement scheme in the well-watered South-west shouldn't work.

His enthusiasm for dairying was perhaps understandable. At that time, Western Australia imported most of its milk products from Victoria and Tasmania. There was no large-scale dairy industry in the West.

The State was then governed largely by men from the same background as Mitchell, rural politicians who saw farmers as the only true producers. Indeed, in Western Australia's primary-based economy, they were almost the only producers of anything. It was also vital to rescue Western Australia from its hourglass image, a mocking metaphor of the low fertility of much of the State's soil.

Mitchell's government had already opened up the Eastern Wheatbelt, clearing vast tracts of land eastwards from the Darling escarpment towards the rainfall limit west of Southern Cross.

Group Settlement was only one of a number of unsuccessful land schemes undertaken throughout Australia in the 1920s. All were based on the assumption that sturdy citizens would eagerly populate and develop virgin land. The eagerness lingered in the minds of politicians long after it had faded for those who were to test their theories.

Like many a subsequent Western Australian Premier, Mitchell was always a man for a project. The Group Settlement Scheme appealed because it appeared to solve several problems. It would alleviate local unemployment, populate the thinly settled forest and south coastal plain, establish a dairy industry and bring migrants from the mother country.

Britain itself, in the grip of economic recession and anxious about its returned soldiers, now out of uniform and often out of work after the Great War, was also keen to export surplus population.

Group settlers.

Mitchell went to London in 1922, his only trip home, and publicised his scheme to all who would listen. He had a good hearing, in both Whitehall and Fleet Street. Several newspaper editors, despite their limited understanding of South-western Australian conditions, did Mitchell's advertising for him. By 1923 Western Australia had loan funds to bring six thousand migrants to the West.

Who came and what were they coming to? Florence Trudgeon, an early arrival from Devon, was one Group Settler whose illusions were short-lived.

> It was in a John Bull *magazine*. And we read it. And they said that within five years you would own your own farm. Well, naturally, we didn't expect to see miles and miles of trees, did we?

Mitchell's optimism was matched only by his energy. He was convinced, and he wasn't alone, that the rich loam which supported the giant karri trees would also nourish lush pasture. If the timber east of the Darling Ranges could be cleared for wheat growing, why not the forests of the South-west? All you had to do was remove the karri.

But the karri proved to be a different proposition from the lighter trees of the Eastern Wheatbelt. An average tree takes four hundred years to reach maturity. By world standards, the karri is massive with towering height and deep roots. But those roots only flourish in deep loam banks, pockets of fertility surrounded by sandier, scrubby soils.

Large areas of the South-west were surveyed and selected for Group Settlement and, despite the warnings of some surveyors about their viability, Mitchell's plans proceeded apace.

John Tonkin, later to become State Premier himself in the 1970s, was a teacher and secretary to a Group Settlement Association near Augusta. He recalls that Mitchell received warning in surveyors' reports, particularly from one who expressed concern about the haste of the operation. Mitchell is reported to have said in reply, 'If they can't find sufficient blocks quickly enough, then

Group settlers, 1920s.

find me those who can!'

Group Settlements were not confined to the far South-west. But the experiences of Group Settlers in the Denmark district, west of Albany, amongst both tall timber and swamp country, offer an insight into the general Group Settler experience.

The various Denmark Groups were comparatively late in the overall scheme. There were many other settlements right through the South-west, including one at Northcliffe in the heart of the karri forest and another at Wellard, where Dorothy Brenton's parents, the Fowlers, first took up land. Their block was not far from the ill-fated site of Thomas Peel's nineteenth-century land settlement. Later the Fowlers were to try their luck in the Denmark area.

The Denmark Group Settlement Scheme began in 1924 when a shipload of some twenty families, many of them from the English West Country, berthed at the port of Albany.

The late Beatrice Whitfield lived to be a vigorous and cheerful one hundred and two. Sitting in her living room in Victoria Street, Albany, in 1983, she told me about her first day in Western Australia. We were looking out across the harbour where she had landed almost sixty years before.

On that day she and her husband travelled west some sixty-four kilometres, across unmade roads to their new home — the Group Settlement camp near the little town of Denmark.

> *Well, we all went up then and found our shack. And we got there with a mud floor, no doors, no windows. And our cup of tea was made of brackish water. Shocking!*

A much younger George Brenton, aged six, also arrived on that ship.

> *I was dressed in cream silk trousers, cream silk shirt. Mum sat me on a black, sawn-off tree stump. And the next thing there was an unholy yell! I got a bull ant bite! But nobody knew what it was! Half the camp was out wondering what had gone wrong.*

George Brenton (left) with his mother and brother, 1923.

Bull ants and brackish water! Nothing very strange to seasoned pioneers, but to immigrants straight from England, startling enough. Several of that first generation of Group Settlers told me that if there had been a boat home they would have jumped on it.

But the irritations and the homesickness were nothing compared with the difficulties posed by the land itself. The coastal country west of Denmark, where the various settler groups were to take up and work their allocations, varied enormously. Along the coastal fringe the country could be swampy whereas the hills to the north were crowned with magnificent stands of karri. Jack Ricketts, a long-time resident of Denmark, still feels that the karri should never have been cut down. The process was wasteful and the timber wasn't put to good use, just ringbarked or burned.

> There was millions of dollars worth of timber just ruined through farming. I think it should never have been used for farming but kept as forest.

Both the swamp and the hardwood country presented problems to the inexperienced. Even in the 1920s, two-men teams of professional foresters took all day to fell a big karri. For the Groupies it was often easier to ringbark the trees and leave them. Some of those splintered grey columns still stand, ghostly memorials to the vanished forest and stark reminders of those early farming failures.

But on the swampy ground, even if the clearing was easier, working the land was just as hard. Beatrice Whitfield's son, Edgar, worked those blocks as a boy.

> You couldn't put a horse on that land. We carted the bags of potato seed on by hand, dug them by hand, carted them off by hand.

Eileen Cross, with her sister Peggy, helped their parents to clear their block.

The kitchen of a Group cottage.

> When the blocks were balloted for, each family went on to their blocks. In our family there were no sons, so the girls had to work. My mother and I had to use a crosscut saw, cut down trees, and my father had a horse and chain. And my father'd cut around a clump of sword grass with a spade and I'd have to hook the chain around it and he'd get the horse. And the horse'd heave and heave till he pulled this sword grass over and we'd go on and spend perhaps half a day doing that. And that's the place to see snakes, tiger snakes at that, when you're in amongst dense, thick, sword grass country. And then there were big banksia trees which had to be sawed down by hand with crosscut saws. Well, today no one would dream of clearing in that way. But that was all that was available in those days, manpower, woman power, horsepower and children power.

Few had farming experience. Laura Mumford and her Yorkshire husband had settled in Denmark well before the Group Settlement Scheme. They saw the first arrivals.

> Well, there was hardly any of them farmers. Our next door neighbour told me one day, 'Do you know the only time I've ever seen a cow is cut up in a butcher's shop!' There was also one Irishman who'd worked at the Guinness Brewery in Dublin. He could make good stout all right but not much else.

The Denmark Group Settlers came from all sorts of backgrounds. One had been a cabinet-maker. George Brenton's father had been a Devon postman. Stan Ravenhill's father, from Gloucestershire, had been a commercial traveller.

Eileen Cross saw her parents and others going to work in the bush.

> Some of them turned up in very bizarre clothing. They still went as though they were going to their office or thought they were

Potato crop, the Cross farm, c1928.

> anyway. They came in their hats and gloves and so forth, and they were handed an axe and a mattock and taken out to the first areas that had been surveyed.

Newly arrived Group Settlers were expected to work together to clear one large tract of land, subsequently divided into individual farms of about ten hectares. Until they could move onto their own property the men were paid three pounds a week sustenance money.

The initial clearing was hard enough. There was little or no mechanised assistance. Slashed ferns grew back over paddocks as fast as they were cleared. And the big trees had to be taken out by hand.

Bill Harrison still chuckles over one tragi-comic effort.

> Well this particular settler, he lived on 139 [Group Settlement No. 139]. And he said, 'I've never seen trees like it in my life'. And he said to his wife, Nellie, to come outside and bring the two children, his two little girls, to watch him fall his first tree with an axe. He got the tree down. But it fell straight across the building. And he said, 'Just as well I got them outside to have a look at the proceedings, otherwise they'd have been flattened too!'

Laura Mumford, with some experience of Denmark farming conditions, thought the Group Settlers seemed driven.

> Everybody was wanting to make something of themselves. They were going so quickly. And farming isn't a thing you can rush. My husband used to say, 'They're going mad! They're going too fast!'

Settlers hoped that, when they took up their own block, the worst would be behind them. But once on their own farm they lost the three pounds a week sustenance money. Now they had to rely

Laura Mumford cooking with a camp oven, 1923.

on what the land could provide. And that was too little.

Ten hectares, even in the well-watered Denmark district, proved insufficient to keep a family going. As George Brenton's family were to find, from hard experience, even if you could feed your family, there was no money left over for farm improvement.

And some of those early warnings about the viability of the land were proving accurate. Jack Brearley's family, at the Northcliffe settlement, for example, had to farm very patchy land with large areas of sandy soil, the cast-offs from the Forestry Department.

And the increasingly depressed conditions of the early 1930s meant that many Groupies were forced off the land they had worked so hard to clear. The early years were, for many, tinged with anxiety.

George Brenton's parents sometimes showed their distress.

> *I can remember Mum going to bed crying because she wouldn't know where the next meal was coming from. And I can remember, as a young, boy getting toed up the seat with Dad's toe. And we reckoned he was a bad-tempered man, but looking back on it now, I think a lot of it was brought on by anxiety and worry.*

And in Eileen Cross's home, there was only bran with which to make bread. Her mother knew it was rough on children's tummies, but she had no choice if they were to eat.

There were also the cultural and social adjustments, not a problem for the children, but a worry for their English parents. When the Cross children wore their boots out, with no hope of replacement, they ran around without shoes or socks like the local kids. For Eileen Cross's mother shoelessness was the ultimate disgrace.

Despite the desperation they sensed in their parents, the children growing up on the Group Settlement blocks found plenty of compensations. The bush, especially to children new from England, was an exciting world of adventure and exploration.

George Brenton and his gang would hide in the scrub,

> *and wait for Charlie Offer with the buggy and his two horses com-*

The Fowler family, c1930.

ing out with the stores. Half a dozen of us used to camp in the bush, in a different spot each time, and wait until the buggy had just gone past and we'd race out and get in underneath the buggy and drag our feet on the white sand because we liked to see the horses really working going up the sand track. And Charlie used to get out with his stockwhip and try to knock us off!

The clearing of the land itself was an adventure for young boys. George Brenton relished the great cubbies that could be made from the huge sheets of bark that came off the ringbarked karri as the pasture was cleared, cubbies that could always be hidden in when there were unpleasant chores to do.

Eileen Cross's sister, Peggy, delighted in the new and exciting environment.

> I think it was a marvellous childhood, because I loved the bush, and I loved cows. And I used to love the milking and anything to do with a horse. I got more than one hiding for riding a horse that I wasn't supposed to. Even the wild brumbies that were out on the coast. I used to go out and catch them and bring them home and then get into trouble for doing so.

Peggy also appreciated her education in the one-teacher schools and the way both teachers and pupils reacted to the rich environment in which they lived.

> Each Friday, instead of having Nature Study in the school, we'd have Nature Study out in the bush. And the teacher'd take us for walks the whole of Friday afternoon. We'd take notebooks with us and write it down. And we'd go right through to Parry's Beach. We'd take our bathers with us. And he taught us all how to swim, in the channel out there.
> Also, as far as the wildflowers were concerned, we used to have a wheel that was made up every month, as the wildflowers came out. We used to bring them to school and we were allowed

Groupies picnic, Parry's Beach, 1920s.

> to draw on this wheel the month and the date when that flower came out. And we had a complete twelve months' record. As a matter of fact I'd love to have that record now of all the wildflowers and orchids that we used to find. It gave us a lot of incentive to look for the flowers so that we could bring them along to draw them on this calendar wheel.

The single-teacher bush schools, which served the Group Settlements, were far from even the nearest country town, and a long way from the head office of the Education Department. They presented challenges to teachers. Lack of materials and resources was often skilfully overcome, as Peggy Cross's wildflower wheel story acknowledges, by imaginative use of the natural environment.

John Tonkin tried to enliven the routine of a school day by exploiting the new technology of radio.

> I went to the trouble of interesting the newly formed Parents and Citizens Association, which we formed in the district, in providing money to install in the school a radio receiver so that I could give a special reward to children by enabling them to listen in to the radio. And it was before broadcasting actually commenced and all we got initially was morse code from the ships round the coast. And I climbed one of the trees in the backyard of the school to put the aerial up so that we could get this.

He was well aware of the value parents placed on pens, pencils and paper, often going without themselves to ensure that their children took the opportunity that schooling offered.

> And some of the children had to ride horses to school, and I had one group of children who came some six or seven miles and they were often the first there.

For the adults too, despite the hard work and the poor returns, there were some compensations. Social life included football

Karridale School, 1926.

(Australian Rules and soccer), cricket and the weekly local dances to which everyone, old and young, turned up.

Laura Mumford was much in demand at the local 'hops' as a skilled pianist and accompanist, and, at ninety years of age, still remembered the dances with delight.

> *Now they were something! And we used to have mouth organs and an accordion, you know, and a rough old floor! But they were the highlights of the week!*

Paddy Cochrane, from Ireland, was one of the accordion players at many a local dance. He obliged me, and some of his bemused neighbours in Denmark, by playing a few of the old melodies.

Sitting on his verandah in Denmark, Paddy, then eighty, began squeezing out 'The Lancers', for the benefit of my tape-recorder, on his well-worn accordion. The elderly couple in the house opposite were delighted. They looked as old as Paddy himself but were obviously just as young at heart. Jigging in time on their front porch, they were soon back in the 1920s.

Everything about those dances, including the music, was homemade and hard-earned. Paddy Cochrane once played so late that

> *one night I got home and I didn't like to make a noise because I hadn't milked my cows. So I thought there's only one thing for it, and that's keep quiet and go home and go to bed. Or else if the cows heard me they'd start roaring and I'd never get to sleep. So I crawled up the paddock and never said a word about it. And the cows never knew I was there.*

But cattle weren't a reliable bet for those would-be farmers in the early years of Group Settlement. A serious and puzzling problem occurred in the Denmark district. Apparently healthy cattle sickened and died on what appeared to be good pasture.

The memory of this unique disaster hasn't faded yet. I have seen many a photograph of emaciated cows, gaunt and staring in

'Deeside Social Orchestra', Andy Boyd, Andrew Adams, Eric Sanders and Charlie Prentis, Northcliffe.

their ringbarked pasture.

In the rush to clear the land in the 1920s, a vital factor had been overlooked. It wasn't until 1933 that cobalt deficiency in the soil was diagnosed. Remedies were applied but too late for some settlers. They had simply given up and moved away.

But it wasn't just the physical and financial hardships that drove many of the Groupies off the land. For those used to the homeliness and close contact of their English villages and towns, the South-west itself, with its tall trees, dense undergrowth, cold, wet winters and isolation from other communities, was a difficult environment. Laura Mumford felt that women, especially, needed neighbours to talk with and to share their experiences.

> *Distances made for a terrible lot. And really in the old settlements it was the womenfolk that could not take it, you know, lack of neighbours and that kind of thing. And in the end a lot of those who left because of the womenfolk.*

And if you were sick and needed attention, it wasn't always easy to get a doctor or any other medical help.

When Paddy Cochrane and his wife needed dental treatment they had to wait for the itinerant dentist. His base was eighty kilometres away in Albany.

> *We arranged to see him when he made a call at a neighbour's place. My wife sat on a log in the bush and he took out a tooth that was giving trouble. Then we both walked the four miles home.*

There were tragedies too. In the Denmark district, Florence Trudgeon and Edith Turner both lost young sons from drinking polluted water in a creek. Some husbands and wives separated as a result of the stress brought about by their new and demanding life. Jack Brearley knew such a family in the Northcliffe settlement.

> *A man and his wife and a young son, he would be about two to*

three years old. And the wife was rather an elegant woman. And I think she had been rather used to the good life. And I'm sure that she just looked at what was offering and told her husband it wasn't on. And very soon afterwards she left and went to Perth.

And, as far as I know, she got a job in Perth. We never saw her again. And he stayed on for a while, her husband, and he just had to battle along on his own. And this led to tragedy in due course.

Suicides, too, were not unknown in the Group Settlements.

But for the most part, people walked off the land either because they were unable to make a living from it or because their previous experience in the United Kingdom hadn't prepared them for life in the Western Australian bush.

To add to their difficulties the country was sliding into the Great Depression of the 1930s, and Western Australia, with its unsophisticated economy based almost entirely on agricultural produce, fared as badly as anywhere.

The Group Settlers had the bad luck to clear their land just in time to see the bottom drop out of the market for almost every kind of produce.

Ironically, dairy farming was to become a reliable source of income in the years following the Depression, years in which a guaranteed milk quota and regular cream cheques began to make up for the grim times the Groupies had gone through.

For those who stayed on, the prizes have gone to the children, if not to the parents. In the Brenton family, of the five sons, only two, George and his brother Sam, are farmers today. In the early 1930s, George, like many men during the Depression, took all kinds of jobs — carting, working in a pub, and mining at Norseman in the Eastern Goldfields.

It was the war which gave him his break. George served with the Royal Australian Air Force (RAAF) in Darwin, gaining a technical training that peacetime would never have given him. After 1945, now married, he and his wife Dorothy acquired a smallholding from the original Group Settlement, worked hard and built it into an efficient mixed farming property of twelve hundred hectares.

For the Brentons at least, it has been possible to say that 'they'd own their own farm'.

But for many others?

I found many former Group Settlers a long way from the scene of their early endeavours. Violet Onions now lives in Fremantle.

> *I'd never want to go through it again, or advise anybody to go through a hard time like that. It wants a lot more thought and consideration before they attempt these things. That was a failure for so many.*

Jack Brearley, then a kid from Yorkshire, lived at the Northcliffe settlement. He has no reservations about that period of his life and reckons that the hard work did him good and helped him mature. It was 'the best apprenticeship I could have had'.

In the long run, Western Australia gained some resourceful people. Undoubtedly the skills they brought with them, even if they weren't useful in the Group Settlement, were to come in handy elsewhere, and if adversity is a good teacher, then plenty of that grit and determination of the stayers in the Group Settlement Schemes have rubbed off onto their children.

But there has certainly been another cost, perhaps one not yet fully recognised.

It is still a daunting sight to drive along the South Coast Highway and see how much karri forest has been cleared along the ridges north of the road, karri forest burnt and cleared by hand over sixty years ago, big timber not likely to ever grow again. The gaunt grey stumps are a lasting memorial to the vanished Group Settlements.

(Based on the ABC Radio documentary broadcast in July 1983)

Groupies, near Denmark, c1924. (Florence Trudgeon is sitting on the left in the middle row nursing her son Henry, Joan Pascoe is on the lap of the woman to the right of Florence, and William Trudgeon is on the far right wearing the cap and holding the dog).

The Cornwall Hotel, Boulder, after the riots, 1934.

A BAD BLUE
The Australia Day Weekend Riots of 1934

You could feel this undercurrent of hostility towards the foreign element, particularly Italians.
        Stella Villa, daughter of an Italian miner.

It was a terrible business. As I say, it's Australia's Day of Shame. It was certainly WA and Kalgoorlie's Day Of Shame.
        Jack Coleman, trade union leader.

A bad blue! That was the general opinion, a bad blue!
        Bronc Finlay, trade unionist.

The events of Australia Day weekend, 1934, in Kalgoorlie can still be regarded as one of Australia's worst displays of xenophobia.

Sydney University historian Ros Pesman has pointed out that, between the two World Wars, Australians visiting Italy outnumbered Italians coming the other way as migrants. Mass migration from Italy came after 1945. But, although their numbers were small at first, Italians were amongst the first people from mainland Europe to try their luck on our shores.

Italian Raffaele Carboni played a prominent role in the Eureka Stockade protest, during the Victorian gold rush, and many other individual Italians came to Australia during the nineteenth century.

In 1891 a contingent of rural workers from northern Italy arrived to cut the sugarcane of tropical Queensland. They were to succeed Kanaka labourers, by then largely repatriated to their original Pacific homes.

Given the contemporary assumption that non-whites were better suited to labour under the tropical sun, the recruitment of Italians to replace Kanakas tells us something of the perceptions of *British* Australians at that time.

Indeed the Italians who came to northern Queensland were referred to sarcastically as 'The Olive Peril'. Similarly unflattering epithets would accompany other Italian migrants over the next fifty years.

In Western Australia, many came in the wake of the Coolgardie gold rush in 1896 and found their way to Gwalia, Boulder, Kalgoorlie and other mining towns.

Still more settled in Perth, or rather its market garden fringes. Some took up rural work further south in the dairy and fruit districts around Harvey and Waroona. Many of these coastal settlers were later to suffer the misfortune of being interned during World War Two.

But for Italians who had made the Goldfields their home, the Australia Day weekend of January 1934 was every bit as traumatic and as bewildering as wartime internment. Evelyn Villa, one of two

The Paizes family, migrants to Kalgoorlie in the early 1900s.

daughters of an Italian miner, sensed her parents' anxiety at the beginning of that troubled weekend.

> *Our Dad, even though he was an Italian, was a naturalised citizen. And we were worried because that seemed to be the people they were against. I was only about ten or eleven at the time, but it's very clear in my mind because it's one of the most horrific experiences I've ever underwent. We came from a very peaceful sort of a home. Our father was northern Italian. Our mother just lived for her husband and the children. It was a very happy household, but you could tell there was something in the air. It was all hushed and quiet. You knew something was about to happen, like, as if a bomb was about to go explode.*
>
> *I know Mum and Dad used to go off and have a chat during this three or four days when all this was happening. And they'd stop their conversation when you came into the room. Yes, you could tell something was about to happen.*

The Villa family were understandably puzzled by the turn of events.

Italians, even though they numbered less than a thousand in all, were part and parcel of Goldfields life by the 1930s, whether as miners, shop owners or hotel keepers. In towns such as Gwalia the men, especially, were celebrated for their music, love of singing, gaiety and good nature.

Kalgoorlie boasted several Italian-run hotels and cafes frequented by Anglo- and Italo-Australians alike.

There was also a substantial Yugoslav population in the twin towns of Kalgoorlie and Boulder. The Slavs, together with the Greeks, who were also part of Kalgoorlie's population mix, were to suffer as much as the Italians from the events of January 1934.

It isn't easy to single out any one cause of the events of that Australia Day weekend, but after four days three men had been killed, many shops, cafes and hotels had been vandalised, looted and burnt. An entire district, home to many Yugoslav and Italian

Hannan Street, after the initial riot, 1934.

families, had been raked with gunfire, homes destroyed and their inhabitants forced to flee, either into the bush, or as far from Kalgoorlie as their feet could carry them.

1934 wasn't the first year in which there had been strife along nationalist lines. Fifteen years earlier a riot had taken place which prefigured its 1934 successor in both its origin and its immediate cause. In 1919 violence broke out after the alleged stabbing by an Italian of a young Englishman, named Northwood, in a street fight.

The mood, in 1919, was ugly, with large numbers of returned soldiers already contemptuous of foreigners and now seeking their old pit jobs back, jobs they believed had been taken from them by Italians while they were away fighting at the front.

That riot was ugly. A few shops were set alight in the anger over the stabbing. Its underlying cause, economic resentment of foreigners, lingered on in Kalgoorlie right through the 1920s and into the 1930s, a prejudice not always expressed openly and rarely expressed against individuals.

It occasionally surfaced in expressions about entire nationalities; Italians were 'Dings' or 'Dagoes', and they stayed that way for half a century and more. There were also overtones of displaced nationalism among the Anglo-Australian population. Australia in the 1920s and 1930s was *British* Australia and all peoples not British were not only less fortunate but less tolerated.

Despite the ominous precedent of 1919, no one would have guessed riots would recur on such a large scale. There was occasional friction but, on the whole, little tension between the various national groups in the Goldfields. Italians and Slavs might be different but they weren't persecuted for being so, and, at a personal level, relations between Italo- and Anglo-Australians could be good. Jack Coleman, as a Miners Union official, knew both groups well, and was surprised by what happened.

> *It's a strange thing really. You could hardly believe this terrible happening was going to take place, because down the mines where I'd worked quite a bit, they were 'Pete' and 'Nick' and so*

on. You'd worked with them, you were good friends and so on!

But despite partnership underground, the Italian and Slav presence in the mines was still unwelcome to some of their fellow miners.

There were complaints that safety standards were compromised by the 'foreigners'' inability to read or understand the printed regulations. In fact, Italians were blamed, rightly or wrongly, for a number of mine accidents in the 1930s.

Italians were also accused of bribing the shift bosses with the notorious 'sling-back' (payment to ensure regular shifts for themselves and their mates). This was particularly resented as the Depression bit deeper and jobs became scarce. Because of the relatively high world gold price, Kalgoorlie suffered less during these hard times than many other Australian communities, but the competition for work was still intense.

The existence of 'sling-back' has always been a matter of conjecture rather than certainty. The practice certainly existed but was not necessarily widespread.

Understandably, many of the Italians I talked to either denied that 'sling-back' occurred or played down its importance. It was common enough at the time in Italy where different labour conditions existed.

Common practice or not, it could have been controlled. As one Anglo-Australian miner put it, 'Why did the shift bosses take the bribes?'

On a social level too, the cultures kept apart. Despite individual tolerance and even friendship underground, at street level the Italian preference for games such as bocce over cricket, and their other, unfamiliar, customs came in for criticism by the Australian majority.

Pud Mann remembers how

Bunches of Italians used to get in the main street outside a hotel, in mobs, and I've seen women have to walk out in the gutter to get around them.

There was room to do so. Kalgoorlie's exceptionally wide footpaths and streets happened to offer more space than those of most Australian towns. And as Yugoslav-born Merinki Levis pointed out, blocking public footpaths wasn't a deliberately offensive gesture, rather the natural behaviour of a society more accustomed to using the street as a social centre.

These resentments aside, normal relationships between Slavs, Italians and other Australians might have continued without undue friction almost indefinitely, but for a fatal combination of circumstances.

Australia Day weekend 1934 began on Saturday, 27 January. It was a hot day, even for Kalgoorlie, and by nightfall the town's many hotels were enjoying a brisk trade.

There was a spate of pub brawls that evening, but one clash became very nasty. It involved an argument between two men, Claudio Mattaboni, barman at the Home from Home hotel in Hannan Street, and Edward Jordan, popular footballer, described by his friends as 'a good man sober but very different with the drink in him'. Their argument began when Mattaboni refused to serve Jordan any more liquor and put him out of the hotel.

The row might have ended then and there but Jordan brooded over his treatment by Mattaboni. Next evening he was back. Again he was refused a drink, this time because he couldn't pay. Argument broke out and once again Mattaboni pushed Jordan from the hotel into the street. He fell back onto the pavement and landed on the back of his head.

He died a few hours later in Kalgoorlie hospital. At the inquest it was found that Jordan had an unusually thin skull and that his fall was the undoubted cause of death. (Mattaboni was later acquitted of the charge of manslaughter.)

Merinki Levis witnessed that fatal confrontation.

> I noticed this scuffle out in front of the hotel, so I just stopped and watched it. I recognised Charlie Mattaboni. It looked like

THE KALGOORLIE MINER, TUESDAY, JANUARY 30.

FATAL ALTERCATION

YOUNG MAN'S DEATH

ITALIAN BARMAN ARRESTED.

On Sunday night, as the result of an altercation between a young man and a barman at the Home from Home Hotel, Kalgoorlie, George Edward Jordan (20), tributer, of Lane-street, Kalgoorlie, died in the Kalgoorlie Government Hospital about 4 o'clock yesterday morning from a fractured skull. Later in the morning Claudio Mattaboni (34), barman, was arrested, brought before Mr. E. McGinn, R.M., in the Kalgoorlie Police Court and remanded on a charge of having unlawfully killed Jordan. Bail was refused.

From reports made to the police, it is stated that an argument arose at the hotel about 7 p.m., in the course of which it is alleged Mattaboni struck Jordan. Deceased left the premises but returned again at about 8 o'clock. The argument was renewed and a fight started on the footpath outside the hotel, during which it is alleged Mattaboni struck Jordan in the face with his fist and deceased fell, striking his head heavily on the pavement. He was removed to the Government Hospital, but his condition was not thought to be serious at the time. However, he passed away about 4 o'clock yesterday morning and a post-mortem examination yesterday afternoon revealed death to be due to a fractured skull.

Although many rumours were in

RIOTING ON THE GOLDFIELDS

DEMONSTRATION AGAINST FOREIGNERS

BUILDINGS LOOTED AND BURNED

REMARKABLE SCENES IN STREETS

Scenes that will long be remembered in the history of the goldfields were witnessed last night by a host of excited spectators, when, as a sequel to the death of George Edward Jordan, who died in the Kalgoorlie Government Hospital at 4 o'clock yesterday morning, from a fractured skull, following an altercation at the Home from Home Hotel, at the western end of Hannan-street, a body of men took the law into their own hands at about 8 o'clock and commenced demonstrations reminiscent of the riots of 1919, when all foreigners were evicted from Kalgoorlie and Boulder, following the death of a young man named Northwood, who was stabbed by a European.

The crowd quickly wrecked three buildings and subsequently set fire to them. In a short while the western end of Hannan-street was a blazing inferno. During the wrecking campaign one constable, who, with others, tried to prevent further damage, was injured and taken to hospital.

The destruction in this quarter having been completed, the men marched along Hannan-street and smashed the windows of several shops belonging to foreigners, leaving a trail of broken glass and wrecked interiors. Kalgoorlie was then almost deserted by the crowd, while they turned their attention to Boulder, where similar scenes were witnessed.

The western end of Hannan-street during the past few years has been largely populated by foreigners, who have made the Home from Home Hotel, conducted by R. Gianatti, and the Kalgoorlie Wine Saloon and gades, to save a dwelling on the western side of the garage, turned their hoses into the flaming mass, amid derisive hoots and jeers of some sections of the crowd. To keep the crowd back,

Report from the Kalgoorlie Miner, 30 January 1934.

> there was an argument there. *This chap was arguing a point with Charlie Mattaboni. Anyhow, he threw a punch at him but missed him. But Mattaboni threw one at him and copped him. And he fell backwards on his head and he just lay there.*

Within hours of Jordan's death rumours flew round Kalgoorlie and Boulder. The lingering prejudices of the 1919 riot, it seemed, were still alive. The story soon got about that Mattaboni had deliberately murdered Jordan. One man was sure Claudio Mattaboni had a knife in his hand, or, as others suggested, more luridly, he had been 'stabbed by a bunch of Italians!'

From then on truth became a casualty. Jordan's death was reported first by word of mouth, and later confirmed in the Monday 29 January edition of the *Kalgoorlie Miner*.

Since police and medical reports had not yet been issued, the newspaper carried no clear explanation of the cause of death. There was no reference to Jordan's skull condition; that would not be known until the Coroner's Report, and not printed in the paper until 2 February. But, equally, there was no suggestion in the *Miner* for 29 January that Jordan's death might have been accidental.

So, in this climate of incomplete information, speculation, half-truth and innuendo prevailed. Rumours fuelled rage. The Jordan family was popular in the town and some were prepared to avenge his death without recourse to law.

Rolf Gerritsen, in his excellent account 'The 1934 Kalgoorlie Riots, A Western Australian Crowd' (*University Studies in History* 1969, Vol. 5, No. 3, Dr J A Merritt and Professor G Bolton), points out that on the Western Australian Goldfields a strong preference for immediate and personal settlement of scores already existed. This factor, together with a combination of anger, alcohol and hot weather, created a dangerous mixture.

It was now the evening of Monday, 29 January.

> *We heard this roar of voices shouting out and we wondered what it was. We didn't know till next morning it was the riots.*

That was how Stanley Davidson, stationmaster at Boulder, almost a kilometre away, heard the first outbreak of anger and violence.

Nancy Crisp lived in the centre of Kalgoorlie and saw the first acts of destruction.

> *We were appalled to see the breaking of bottles, furniture and furnishings being thrown over the balcony, and then of course the flames. There were cars, which were not very numerous then, flying down the street, with people singing and shouting, which amidst the trouble of those whose homes and hotels had been sacked, was rather appalling to the rest of us.*

Stationmaster Stanley Davidson caught up with the damage next morning when he came up the Golden Mile from Boulder.

> *There was one particular cafe. This place was smashed to smithereens, and there was ice cream and fruit all out the front. And over the door was this caption. I'll always remember this. It was called The Green Bar, this milk bar, and it said: 'Bring your sweetheart to the Green Bar!' And it looked so futile to see this caption there.*

So where were the police? Before the disturbance started no special security precautions had been taken and when the riots began there was not a strong police presence. Had there been, events might have turned out quite differently. Apparently, the inspector in charge, a Mr McDonald, did not believe that there would be any trouble after Jordan's death. However, one of his deputies, Police Constable Eric Sunter, was more sceptical.

Knowing that he could not control an angry mob by himself, Sunter stepped out of uniform and quietly patrolled the streets, making personal notes about offences and offenders. His discreet and careful observations were to bring at least some of the rioters to justice a few days later.

Merinki Levis confronted two of the offenders himself.

> *I walked up the street with a couple of friends. And there was a Yugoslav there named Mick Vilatich. He had a barber's shop there and they broke the doors and were filling up their shirts with cigarettes, hair oil, anything they could get hold of. And there were two detectives standing out the front and I said to them, 'What are you doing standing there? Why don't you stop this?' And he said, 'Listen mate! If you want to go in there and get your head blown off, you go in!' Well, you know we walked in! And they all walked out. There'd have been at least ten or twelve of them in there. They just moved further up the street. But as you were seeing what they were doing, burning this down and filling up their shirts with grog, with cigarettes and crayfish, it made you cry really to see what was going on.*

With hindsight, it is doubtful whether the town's small police force could have coped with what was rapidly becoming a major civil disturbance. Kalgoorlie was a long way from other centres of population. Train travel from Perth took the best part of a day. Even if reinforcements had been sent immediately they would have been too late to deal with the first and second violent nights of the riot.

When the police did arrive four days later they were too late. The violence was over. The effectiveness of these reinforcements was also questionable. Kalgoorlie townspeople recognised some of the hastily recruited 'specials' as ex-petty criminals, recruited in desperate circumstances.

But, whether as specials or experienced police, they would have had to deal with a major civil emergency. Law and order had broken down completely in the main streets.

Even the efforts of the Kalgoorlie Fire Brigade were sabotaged. Rioters grabbed the firemen's axes and slashed their hoses while hotels and houses burnt fiercely in front of them.

Kalaf Brothers Cafe, after the riots, 1934.

One of Marjorie Henderson's two brothers took part in the looting of shops and came home with his booty. But not for long.

> *He had a bottle of whisky and one of those three-cornered, big, heavy ashtrays. And my father was furious. And he took them out onto the woodheap and he smashed them with the axe, the bottle of whisky and the ashtray. And he forbade my brother to leave the house. Dad told him he could go to gaol for that. He said, 'Can't you wake up to yourself!'*

That could have been said of many others that night. Evelyn Villa saw the next, even uglier, phase of the riot.

> *The rioters were not only happy to burn the big hotels in Kalgoorlie and then to do the same in Boulder. But then they decided to participate in the destruction and the burning of the everyday family homes there, irrespective of whether they were Greek, Italian, German, Yugoslavs, whatever. They were all classified as Dings. And their idea was to get rid of the Dagoes. They didn't want a bar of them!*

Tuesday morning, 30 January, dawned on a scene of desolation, devastation and fear in Kalgoorlie. Hotels, cafes and shops still smouldered, while their contents, or what was left of them, littered the pavements. All this had been the work of a hundred or so drunken men and, in their wake, looters looking for easy pickings.

Nancy Crisp's mother knew one of the Italian hotel licensees well.

> *She went up to her and she saw her standing in the street, almost in tears and staring at the still smoking ruins of the hotel. And she went up to her and just put her arms round her. But you could hardly tell a person you were sorry their home had been burnt down, deliberately, could you? And Mrs Fiori said, 'I didn't think they'd do it. I didn't think they'd do it to me!'*

Special constables parade in Perth before leaving for Kalgoorlie, 1934.

Many felt a similar sense of disbelief. Men who were naturalised Australians suddenly found themselves hated foreigners.

Nancy Crisp observed that as the Italians in their street began to make plans to deal with this crisis, they remained unfailingly polite to those Australians they knew and trusted. But at the same time, their families were already hiding valuables, often with Australian friends, and making plans to leave Kalgoorlie as soon as possible before matters got worse.

Normally, after the Australia Day weekend, it would have been business as usual at the mines. But on this Tuesday the men working at Kalgoorlie's largest mines, the Lake View and Star, stopped work and held a meeting. They wanted to talk about Jordan's death and sort out some of the problems they were having with the migrant workers. The miners resolved not to go back to work unless management assured them that no foreign workers would go down the mine with them. Their action was swiftly followed by workers elsewhere along the Golden Mile.

The riot was now bringing to the surface long suppressed resentments, against foreigners in general and their work practices in particular. Union officials and some union members found themselves powerless to deal with these prejudices.

Not all the miners or their delegates held anti-Italian or anti-Slav views. In fact the left wing of the union, represented by officials like Jack Coleman and Bronc Finlay, urged the men to direct their grievances against the mine managers rather than at their 'foreign' fellow workers.

In vain they tried to point out that the employers were taking advantage of widespread unemployment to pay low wages and, in the same spirit, ignore safety standards.

But Edward Jordan's funeral was to be held that day, and would be the most heavily attended funeral ever seen on the Goldfields. The miners were in no mood to listen to industrial arguments.

This was evident later in the afternoon, at a mass meeting in

'Cleanliness and Civility', looted shop window, Kalgoorlie, 1934.

Boulder. Jack Coleman had spent the entire day urging action against management rather than migrant miners.

> *Several hundred people turned up at this little grassy spot with a rotunda on it. And on the rotunda there was a bunch of politicians, local AWU [Australian Workers' Union] officials up there, putting on a pitiful exhibition, agreeing and not agreeing with what was in hand; absolutely, in my terms, gutless. There was no clear statement! Leftist radicals were excluded, those who wanted to tell the miners to go back home and go to work.*
>
> *And they just stood there. Jelly! Jelly! They were just shaking. They didn't know what to do.*
>
> *'Yes, yes, yes, you won't have to work with them! The buying of jobs has got to stop!' And so on.*
>
> *The only people to stand up, to hand out leaflets telling the miners not to fight against their fellow workers but to fight for shorter hours and not to differentiate against the foreign-born workers, was a handful of leftists, of which I was one, giving out these leaflets. But oh! they disregarded them. Some read them obviously. One bloke made a heap of them and burnt them in the gutter, near the pay store. I always remember that. One of the pay stores was set alight!*

But even as that meeting at Boulder was debating these issues, the miners' arguments were interrupted by the sound of small-arms fire and explosions. The noise came from nearby Dingbat Flat, the local name for a large gently sloping area east of Boulder railway station.

Dingbat Flat, with its filter-press humpies and ramshackle galvanised cottages, housed over a hundred Italian and Slav families. Their breadwinners, fearing a repeat of Monday night's violence, had armed themselves against any likely attack on their homes and families.

It wasn't hard, in a mining town, to obtain explosives and most men knew how to use them. Jam-tin bombs filled with grapeshot

Dingbat Flats ablaze, 1934.

were handy enough weapons. The immigrants' precautions were soon justified.

That evening, during the Boulder miners' meeting, a dozen or so rioters launched an attack on Dingbat Flat. They were repelled with weapons from the home-made arsenals.

Infuriated by this vigorous defence, those not injured by flying fragments went off in search of arms, even checking out the police station as a source of supply. Eventually they rounded up enough rifles to return and renew their assault.

So the battle of Dingbat Flat began. Stanley Davidson saw how it ended.

> They ran up there. They raided this place. They hunted all the women and children out, who, more or less, took to the bush for protection. And they razed the place to the ground. You could see burnt-out homes and sewing machines and wirelesses. It was a sorry sight.

Stanley's wife, Patience, watched the sequel, the migrant exodus from Boulder.

> These women, they were all in black, every one of them, and they were just, you know, with their hands clasped, just looking up, in prayer, and crying! The tears running down their faces, little children hanging on to their skirts. At that time I said a short prayer to God that it would end soon because it was terrifying.

Wednesday, 31 January, was another hot summer day.

By now many Italian and Slav families had fled to the bush or left town altogether. Merinki Levis provided food and shelter for some two hundred refugees in his family's market garden outside the town boundary. But even the sight of his vehicle, returning from town with supplies for them, induced fear and panic among many of the refugees. Others, less lucky, had hidden in the bush

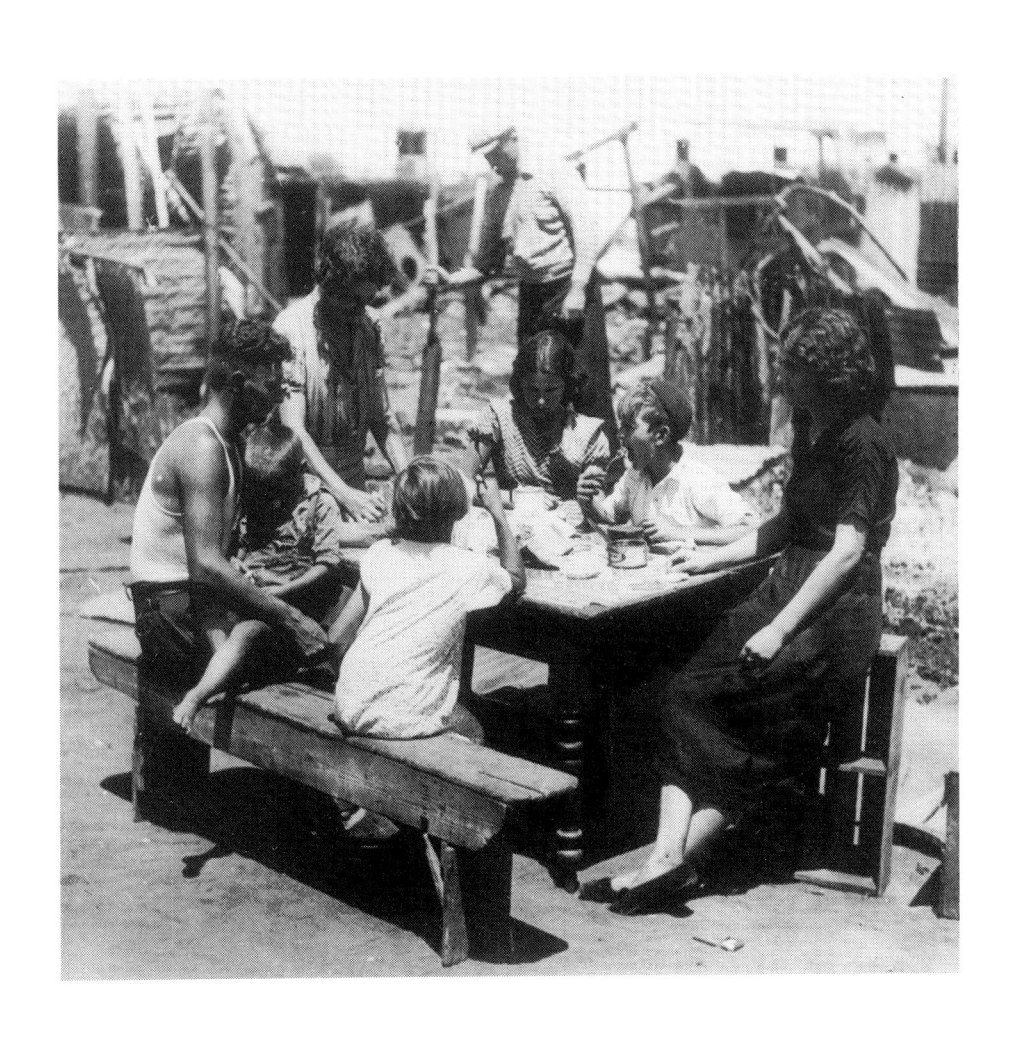

Family meal among the ruins, Kalgoorlie, 1934.

and stayed there for days afterwards, unwilling to accept any assurance that the riots had spent their force. Red Cross helpers who went out with water and supplies for several days after the riots got the same fearful reaction. The refugees thought these samaritans had come to kill them.

Back in Kalgoorlie itself, Stella and Evelyn Villa were told by their parents that they must get ready to leave quickly.

> *Dad was very worried at the time. He said, 'Well, we'll leave!' The neighbours were very good. Actually they were all Australians, apart from one Italian family across the road. They shifted any furniture of value out of our home, put it in different homes. They filled the car and we set off. And right along the road from Kalgoorlie, almost all the way to Southern Cross [a distance of almost 150 kilometres] there were people walking like so many refugees, their bundles on their backs, little children walking along with their mothers, holding their hands. It was pretty grim!*

It has to be acknowledged that many ordinary Australians were deeply affronted by what had happened. Although they were powerless to do much to stem the violence and destruction, many were still able to prevent further injury and suffering by offering help and shelter to the victims.

Beatrice Wellington's family helped out in this way. Her mother, who kept a shop in Boulder, hid one man under her bed, while outside, two burly Slavs kept watch on her property in case the rioters tried to set a 'safe house' alight.

Strangely, the violence petered out as suddenly as it had flared up in the first place. By Thursday, as men sobered up and looked around at what had happened, there was a growing sense of self-reproach among the miners themselves.

Yugoslav Joe Katich was one of two men killed in the battle of Dingbat Flat. An Anglo-Australian, Charlie Stokes, was the other.

Katich's funeral, on Thursday, like Jordan's two days earlier, was

Cianatti's Home from Home Family Hotel, Kalgoorlie, after the riots, 1934.

well attended and not just by Slavs. Several hundred Anglo-Australians turned up to pay their last respects.

Kalgoorlie made international news that week. Both the British and the Italian press made much of the riots, and from Rome, Benito Mussolini sent compensation (to the tune of one hundred pounds sterling) for the victims of the violence.

The Western Australian Government also offered recompense. After bringing some of the offenders to justice, the State provided relief accommodation for the displaced families and, later, new homes for those who chose to remain on the Goldfields.

Not that many of the migrants had much choice. Their best hope of work in 1934 was still in the gold industry.

By Monday morning, 5 February, the mines were back in production. Men who had rioted and looted went back underground with fellow workers whose families they had terrified and whose homes they had destroyed.

Jack Crisp described the mood in the aftermath of the riots.

> Oh, there was a great deal of bitterness. I was working underground at the time. The Australians, Italians and Slavs were a mixed force underground. Things were very unhappy for quite a while.

Pud Mann saw the whole episode as a sequence of events which got out of control.

> I don't think it was hatred, just alcohol. Some of the places they burnt down, they used to work with the same chaps underground.

Stella Villa still reflects on those four days of violence.

> Children accept things such as births and deaths more than grown-ups and you learn to accept these things. But I was devas-

STRANGE BURIAL SERVICE

FUNERAL OF JOSEPH KATICH

Three hundred coatless, dust-begrimed foreigners marched through the dust and heat to the Boulder cemetery yesterday to join in one of the strangest funeral ceremonies held on the goldfields in recent years. They had come in from their places of refuge in the bush surrounding Boulder and Kalgoorlie to carry out the last wishes of their comrade, Joseph Katich, who was killed in the battle between rioters and foreigners at the foot of the Ivanhoe dump on Tuesday night. Katich had left a will, made before he underwent an operation on January 16, in which he asked his closest friend to see that no religious rites should be observed when he was buried. His fellow countrymen met before the funeral arrangements were made and agreed that his wishes should be carried out. It was decided that he should be given a worker's burial.

At 5 p.m. his friends from among the foreign population, and a few of his British workmates, gathered at the Boulder undertakers where his body lay, and a few minutes later the black-draped coffin bearing Katich's remains was placed in the hearse and the funeral procession, formed of dusty, tired-looking men, marching four abreast, started. A cloud of red dust marked the route of the funeral cortege as it made its way through the heat on the journey to the cemetery. Five motor car loads of mourners followed.

At the graveside, Katich's closest friend explained deceased's last wishes to the mourners, and added in his own tongue that Katich had not wanted to die, but that when the call came he had been happy to die in the defence of his home. He then delivered a funeral oration in the Dalmatian tongue and concluded by calling for three cheers for the dead man. They were given in ringing tones.

Other speakers of different nationalities followed with tributes delivered in their own languages. All referred to the deceased as a humble working man who had been killed because of the ferocity of a misguided few. Cheers were called for and given at the conclusion of each tribute. A compatriot of the dead man, who spoke in English, said that Katich had died beloved of all Jugo Slavs. He had always been a working man with a worker's ideals, and he had died in the defence of those ideals. An invitation was then given for any Britisher present to deliver an address. A young miner came forward and said that Katich had been one of his best friends. His death had been brought about by the acts of a few irresponsible fools and every sane man on the 'fields was very sorry for the whole affair. The people of Boulder, he said, would help the sufferers from the rioting to rebuild their homes.

A Communist then took the opportunity of delivering a typical propaganda speech, but several of Katich's friends stated that he had never been a Communist.

The coffin was then lowered into the grave and the strange funeral ceremony ended. Most of the foreigners present then returned to their hiding places in the bush, although a policeman assured them that they would receive police protection if they remained in the township.

Report from the Kalgoorlie Miner, 2 February 1934.

tated to think that people who call themselves human beings could act so unkindly towards other people who hadn't done anything wrong.

It was, as trade union official Bronc Finlay said, 'a bad blue'.

(Based on the ABC Radio documentary broadcast in April 1986)

Dingbat Flats, c1934.

Job Seeker, late 1930s.

STONYBROKE AND WALKING
Memories of the Great Depression

You do sink down. It's no good saying, 'Well, I'll only go this far down'. You're right on the skids all the time.

The late Richard Beilby, novelist and former swaggie.

Richard Beilby was one of hundreds who took to the roads searching for work, food and shelter in a decade when Australia bore its share of world-wide Depression.

It is generally conceded that the Great Depression of the 1930s hit Australia harder than most countries, and perhaps Queensland, Western Australia and South Australia were more affected than most States in the Commonwealth.

Western Australia suffered from a lack of economic diversity. John Tonkin, later to become Labor Premier in the 1970s, saw the Depression at close quarters. It was part of his political and economic education. In the 1920s he was secretary to Group Settlers in the South-west, helping migrant farmers with their bookkeeping, and later, as the State Member for Fremantle, he knew the level to which many people were reduced.

> *You see there was very little else in Western Australia. And the people were dependent upon the produce from the land, wheat and sheep, and the shipping which was generated to take the wheat and wool away. Now in North Fremantle itself, there was scarcely a home where there wasn't someone out of work. And in some homes everybody was out of work.*

The situation in the rural areas was just as bad, especially in the hastily cleared country east of the Darling Ranges, land intended as the breadbasket of the State. The Western Australian Wheatbelt and its supporting rail freight network now stretched inland to Southern Cross, right to the very edge of the marginal rainfall area. This vast area promised both grain for export and a good income for farming families looking for new land.

But when the price of wheat fell, the hopes and hard work of several years went with it. Most farming people were reduced to subsistence.

Clee Jenkins, who later became a distinguished entomologist and rural commentator, has personal memories of their situation. At that time he was a young clerk working for the Agricultural Bank.

Richard Beilby (left) and Tom Dundee, washing day on the track, Yarraloola Station.

> People were absolutely devastated by the conditions under which they were living. They had no ready money at all. They were issued credit by the Agricultural Bank, later the R & I [Rural and Industries] Bank. I think the amount given to a single person was three pounds a month, and a married couple, I think, had four to five pounds a month. That was in credit, not hard cash. And there were instances of people who just hadn't got enough money even to buy a postage stamp.

The plight of farming families was all the more poignant because they had been encouraged to clear huge tracts of scrub and forest. In the late 1920s, wheat still looked like the boom crop of the future. In 1929, Norman Lockyer, then farming in the Avon Valley, saw

> dozens and dozens of the new AL harvesters going up on the train to the new wheat areas which had been thrown open in the previous five years. But in 1931 to 1932 they were all coming back again. They had been repossessed.

Some farm and stock sales were black-banned by fellow farmers. No one would bid for their neighbours' possessions. But they sometimes clubbed together, bought up some of the farmer's chattels and handed them back to the unlucky family, a practice that has recurred in rural Australia in the early 1990s.

In some accounts of the 1930s, the banks are depicted as the villains of the piece, foreclosing on farmers when they could have extended credit. But it is probably only fair to acknowledge that bank officers on the spot had no real control over events, just as Australia itself was powerless to dictate its own terms in an internationally depressed market. Relations between bank officials and farmers could be humane and considerate.

Clee Jenkins witnessed one meeting between banker and client.

Soup kitchen, Melbourne.

> There was a lot of amazing stoicism among the farmers who stayed. I had lunch with one man at Campion, which is just near the rabbit-proof fence, along with the bank manager, who was doing his level best to help these people. And I said, in my innocence, in those days not having a great experience of the Wheatbelt, 'Why do you stay if conditions are so bad?' The man looked at me and said, 'Well, my daughter, aged fourteen, actually cooked and dressed this sheep which we're eating. And the sheep belongs to the bank. We could not raise the fare for all the family to go to Perth, if we wanted to go. And when we got there we would have nowhere to go, and at least we have a roof over our head and we will stay here.'

Another bank employee, Ted Johnson, later a Labor member of the State Parliament, saw how the sudden loss of income affected not just the farmers but those who worked for them.

> People who had employees on the farm were told, on more than one occasion, that they couldn't afford to pay wages. And I know of several cases where head office said he cannot afford to carry anyone at all.
>
> And the chap would say, 'Well, Joe has been with me three years. He's a darn good worker, I can't turn him out on the road with nothing!' And the bank manager would say, 'Well, head office says you've got to! The only thing I can suggest is that you can't pay him wages. But there's no reason why you shouldn't keep him on if he's agreeable, and when you come to town at the weekend, give him a bit of tobacco, let him have a few beers as you would your family.'

The men and women I interviewed in recording material for 'Stonybroke and Walking' came from a wide cross-section of society and from both city and country, but wherever they came from and however hard or lightly the Depression dealt with them, it was not material deprivation but loss of morale and the defeat of the human

Sunday morning, sustenance camp, Boyup Brook.

spirit that they remembered most strongly.

Violet McCashney's husband was a builder and a skilled craftsman. Like many other men he was out of work for much of the 1930s. Violet's most abiding memory of those times was denial of dignity.

> *People do try to belittle you. And that's always been a great thing with me. I can't stand people to be belittled.*

Annie Evans, of Bassendean, whose husband, Arthur, was out of work for much of the 1930s, had been saving up for her marriage.

> *And I had worked solid for seven years and I had been very fortunate. I had gathered up linen and kitchen utensils – and I had a big packing case, what I call a glory box. And my husband broke it all up and made shelves either side of a secondhand bed we bought for twelve and six. And I put curtains up and he put his clothes in one side and I had mine in the other.*

Joan Fletcher came from a farming family. They had to walk off the farm when the bank foreclosed on her father in the early 1930s. The bank took their furniture. They left their home with a few personal effects and the clothes on their back.

Eventually her mother was able to make ends meet for the family by running a boarding house. But her father took their loss very hard.

> *I think it broke his heart. He was a farmer from a very young man. From then on he had very poor health. He had been very healthy until then. He had to go rabbit trapping. He had to go clover rolling for the farmers around the district, whom he had been equals with.*

The writer Richard Beilby regarded the Great Depression, along with World War Two, as the most formative experience of his life.

Joan Fletcher (left) and friend, Show Day, 1935.

For him and many others the Depression was a kind of odyssey, but with no sight of Ithaca, tramping the back roads in search of ever-elusive work and, if nothing else, food and shelter.

When Richard Beilby left school in the late 1920s the only work he could get was the occasional stint with a shearing team up north. Otherwise it was the open road, the railway yard or the sustenance camp until he and the army accepted each other gratefully in 1938.

The Depression taught him how to share a tent with eight other men, and live rough on poor rations, experience that served him well when World War Two came and he soldiered in the Middle East and Crete.

Dorothy Brooks of Fremantle, as a young mother in the 1930s, walked the streets

> *trying to find sixpence to pick up to go to the butcher's and buy a shank for the baby's broth. And that's the sort of thing I did. And I never found any. But I found a friendly butcher who used to give me the biggest one he could find.*

For those who lived in the country or in country towns, the phrase 'living off the land' acquired a literal meaning. There were no jobs and no cash.

Mort Ewing was a teenager in the coastal town of Augusta. For him the Depression meant living off the sea

> *selling fish. The people of Augusta used to make their living out of that and often they'd be out working, in pairs of course, and they would come to us and say, 'What are you doing tonight?' And we'd say, 'Nothing!'*
>
> *'Right! Be ready at half-past six. We'll go out netting. A third for you and a third for me and a third for the boat.' Well you go out and I don't know if you've ever experienced what it's like to be out hauling a net in the middle of winter, wet to the skin and hopping out into water up to your chest and then hauling a fish net three or four hundred yards up the beach. And the cold*

Slum housing, Collingwood, 1936.

> water'd be running up your arms as you put it back on the net-
> board. And you'd get terrific pains in the stomach from the
> intense cold. And I earned 1/8d. That was one shilling and
> eight pence for nine hours' night work in the freezing cold.

Hardships of a different kind were just as keenly felt in the city.

Violet McCashney's husband walked the streets and suburbs of Perth in search of work of any kind. For the McCashneys there was only the wry consolation that they were both young and that

> When you've got other people in the same box, you make a bit
> of a joke of it. You say, well, I can't afford butter, so we'll just
> eat dripping. And dripping was the mainstay of life in those
> days.

Clothing too was a continuous problem.

> I was often handed down men's serge trousers to make up for my
> son. I made his trousers right up till he was nine, lined them
> with flour bags. You'd often find the printing on the inside of
> the trousers. I never bought any clothes for five years I suppose.

Annie Evans knew numerous families where, to make a living, many men took to cutting timber in the bush and selling it for firewood — a task that came her way too:

> And you had to turn round and get the axe and split it down
> and chop it. My husband was away in the sustenance camps
> and I had to do that myself. So did a lot of the women. And
> then he'd be home for three or four weeks without money. He'd
> send me money but he had to have some to keep him going
> down there. And when he came home we'd live on that, sparing,
> and then he'd go back again and I'd have to wait for a fort-
> night's wages for him to send me what he had. I paid rent. I
> used to pay twelve shillings and sixpence a week for a rented

Sustenance camp, Western Australia, c1931.

> house. That came out of the wages. I went to the baker and the butcher and the grocer used to come around and you'd get the bare necessities. Many's the time I was only left with two shillings. You couldn't go to the pictures or any entertainment because you didn't have the wherewithal. And my Mum and Dad were struggling too. And you couldn't ask for help so you just put up with it.

Annie Evans' family experience was not untypical. Her parents were migrants from Scotland who had come to Australia in the hope of a better life. Her two brothers found only occasional farm work at seven shillings and sixpence a week. Annie's husband, Arthur, also a migrant from the United Kingdom, spent much of the 1930s in working camps for the unemployed.

And yet when I first started to record Depression experiences, I found that some people who had lived through the 1930s were scarcely aware of the Great Depression. Family funds had sustained them through these difficult times but such folk were the exception rather than the rule. Most people felt the Depression personally and recalled it as the most socially and politically formative experience of their lives.

A particular problem in Western Australia was the loss of export income from the economic mainstay, farm products. This collapse produced a domino effect on the rest of the economy. Supply and service industries and retail stores were all affected so that the State Government found itself dealing with both blue-collar and white-collar unemployment on a large scale.

How could work be found for so many who needed it? Various schemes were put into action.

Sixty years on, one of the most visible is the Harvey drainage scheme, which still serves the dairying district of the South-west, and across much of the countryside large gangs of city-bred men were sent out to dig drains or mend roads.

The Government was determined to get unemployed men out of the capital, a resolve accelerated by fear of social unrest. Workless

Unemployed march to register for assistance, Melbourne.

men, hanging around Perth, could take it into their heads to challenge the system, a system that had cost them their pride and their hope.

Those who went to work in the country were housed in the notorious sustenance camps. The novelist the late Donald Stuart felt they were places where

> *men worked and sat idle, did useless work for one week out of three. They lived in soggy tents. They did some worthwhile work I suppose. They drained a few swamps, they dug a few ditches. But it was all soul-destroying, disheartening.*

One of those sustenance camps — Blackboy Camp — lay just to the east of Perth, in the Darling Ranges. Men were sent there, it was said, to be 'out of sight of the better-off'.

Annie Evans recalls the effect of Blackboy Camp:

> *A lot of them got very devastated there. They sort of couldn't take it, you know. A lot of them couldn't face up to the heavy manual work. Some of them went up to farms. And they were told, 'Oh, get off from here!' They had no idea of farms! And then they'd go back on the tickets!*

Later, her own husband was sent to work clearing in the big timber around Manjimup.

> *And he wouldn't take me down there because he said it was a pleasure to be able to get out of that and come home. He hated the loneliness of sitting in the camp, he read a lot, but there was no entertainment — and that's the type of life he and many more put up with. If he was in an area where there were a lot of men there'd be rows of tents, and it wasn't so bad, but when they were clearing the single blocks around they were on their own. He was very bitter about the conditions down there, especially in the wintertime. He used to be out working all day, take his crib*

Sustenance workers, Fremantle, c1931.

> with him, billy of cold tea and he would come home a night to
> find his camp all wet, his bed wet and everything, and he'd
> leave his billy swinging on the camp fire outside. That'd be all
> down in the ashes, wild cats had got to it, or they'd got into his
> camp, they could smell food in there and they'd turned his safe
> upside down.

The unemployed were not always young and sprightly. Many had sat for years in office chairs and were unfit for sustained manual work.

Joan Fletcher saw the outcasts arrive in the South-west.

> Sometimes in the middle of the night they would be dropped off
> at Cranbrook or Boyup Brook. This was in winter, pouring rain.
> They'd get out there and have to put up their tents. Now the
> tent poles'd be thrown on the ground. They'd be given a tent
> and they'd have to start a new life and it would be very difficult
> if you didn't know how to put a tent up. You'd maybe worked in
> a shop and suddenly you were confronted with a new way of life
> and you had to find a new way of life for yourself.

At one stage Mort Ewing was in charge of a road gang of unemployed men. It was especially hard, he felt, for the older ones.

> They would come to me, some of them, and say, 'Oh! I've got a
> bad back' or 'I'm very sick!' And I wasn't in a position to say,
> 'Don't work!' But not being a cruel sort of person, I used to fix
> them up with jobs where I couldn't see them and nobody else
> could see whether they worked or not.

For young men like Richard Beilby and Donald Stuart the 'susso' camps were too depressing to linger in. Perhaps they saw in the tired faces of the older men there a grim mirror of their own fate if the bad times persisted.

It was Donald Stuart who quoted the plodding rhyme from

On the track in search of work.

which I took the title for the radio programme.

> *What's the use of talking!*
> *when you're stonybroke and walking.*
> *And the Blucher boots are squeaking*
> *and the waterbag is leaking.*
> *And you're tramping in a creek bed*
> *ninety miles from anywhere.*

And in Richard Beilby's time on the road,

> *In almost every country town, you'd find the hoboes camped.*
> *They used to call us hoboes. You'd always find us camped down*
> *by the standpipe, where the railway engine tanks were filled up.*
> *There were always big lumps of coal there too so there'd be a fire*
> *going, and possibly two, three, half a dozen men sitting round it*
> *with their gear. You'd walk in. And there was a lot of informa-*
> *tion passed around there.*

The talk was about where jobs or food might be found. The railway shed walls also spoke. They were a cryptic billboard for the unemployed, with messages at once functional and confidential. Bill Hampton got to know the language well.

> *There was a system of code marks and everybody understood them.*
> *Don't go to that house. You'll get no food. These are good people.*
> *You'll get food. That's what they literally meant. These were in the*
> *railway sheds where people'd get coal. They'd put up information,*
> *where there was a good bite and which was a bad bite.*

Despite the universal hardship, or perhaps because of it, there was compassion for the battlers and the luckless. Donald Stuart appreciated that, although they were little better off than many of their customers, many storekeepers would give credit if they could. Others would offer food for work.

> *We went to the local baker in the Goldfields towns, in the North-west towns. And we said, 'G'day Bake! Any chance of chopping some wood for a staley?' And he'd give us a stale loaf and say, 'Well look! I've had twenty blokes here in the last two days chopping wood for me. And there's no wood left to chop.'*

Perhaps the most poignant story I heard was Bill Hampton's *near perish* in north-east Queensland. And if you find it moving to read this, I can assure you that the original spoken word is even more powerful, not least because Bill Hampton himself could not remember the humanity shown to him without deep emotion.

> *There was dozens and dozens of us all trying to get a job and he used to say, 'Come back tomorrow! Come back tomorrow! Come back tomorrow!'*
>
> *And that lasted three days. So in absolute hunger and desperation I went along to the men's mess and tried to buy some food off the proprietress. And the poor woman nearly cried! She said, 'Look son, I've given that much food away, I'm losing money'.*
>
> *So I walked. I can't think of the distance, into Cardwell. And there was a wonderful Greek woman who ran a restaurant there, and I decided just to walk in, sit down, have a meal, eat all I could and just say, 'Ring the police!' And when I walked in, she could see it, my youth and my desperation, she could spot it. When I sat down she come up. 'Son', she said, 'you haven't eaten for days!' And she heaped everything she could, until I nearly fell asleep on the plate!*

Richard Beilby was also well aware of compassion for his fellow outcasts.

> *There was a lot of comradeship, and that's a very much misused word these days, or mateship, and it definitely did exist. And my*

experience of it in the Depression and in the army is that it was born out of adversity.

Adversity also bred survival skills. To find work or food you had to know how to get around. Mostly that meant walking, but if you were lucky you could 'jump the rattler', take a train to the next town along the line. Bill Hampton was a frequent 'rattler jumper'.

Timing or 'taking it on the fly' was all important. It meant that you

> got out [preparing yourself to jump on to the train] *near the signal lamps and before the train speeded up and you had to go over the side. If it was too fast you couldn't make it. You got splinters in your hands. You lost your swag, because the first thing you did was throw your swag in and you jumped on the side. And if you didn't make it, your swag was gone and all your belongings.*

Even if you made it over the side, your problems weren't always over. Or perhaps they were! There were always

> *the police. If you were under the canvas in the rattler, they would move along, if the train stopped and they'd say, 'Is there any room in there mate? You got any room in there?'*
>
> *And if you were innocent enough to reply, 'Yes mate, hop in here!', out of compassion for a fellow rattler jumper, they'd say, 'Right mate! Out mate! C'mon!' And this didn't worry you because if you were starving you at least had forty-eight hours of food from the police station.*

Donald Stuart took one very rough ride in the Northern Goldfields.

> *I got into an empty truck full of coaldust, straws and all sorts of rubbish, stretched out and just above Cue a particularly fierce*

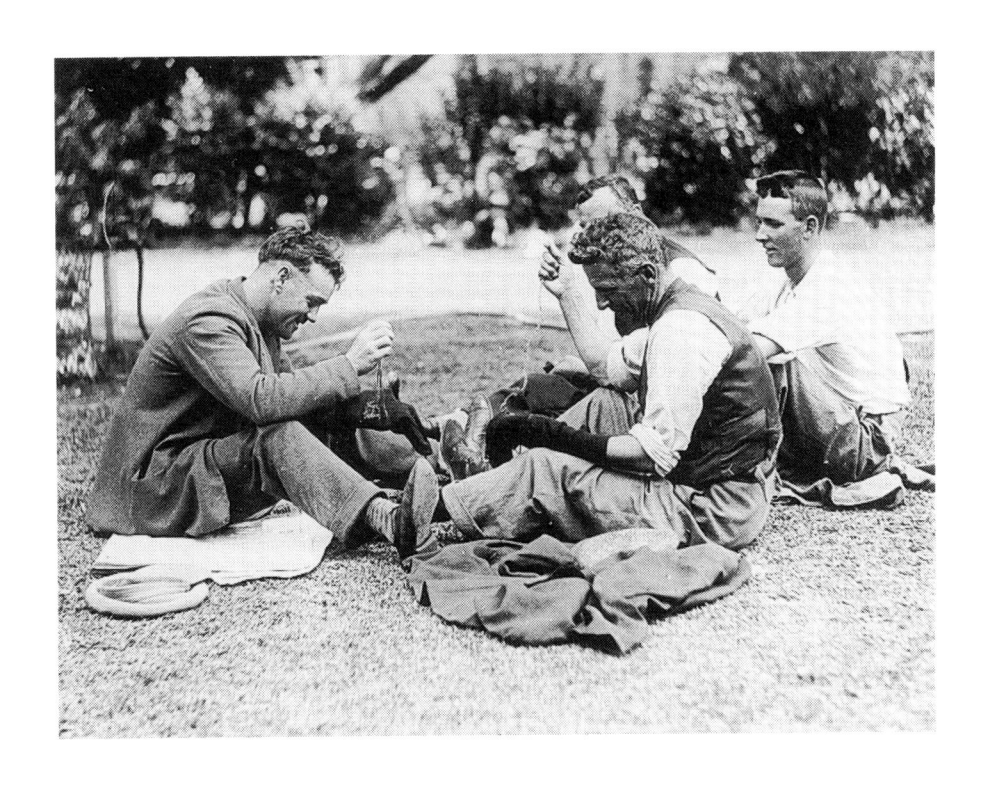

Unemployed mending clothes, 1930.

and heavy downpour of rain caught me. And I thought, Well, it's a nice old bloody business, isn't it, when a man makes a successful train jump and the Good Lord sends down heavy rain and there's no getting away from it.

For men, when work came at last, after a decade of continuous unemployment, it was hard to settle down to a nine-to-five routine. For those who had filled their days by fishing or living off the land, paid employment was monotonous.

For women not part of the paid workforce, the struggle to keep families fed and clothed, without the support of their absent husbands, took a continuous toll. For those put out of work, it was also the war which would offer them their next regular employment, in munitions or military clothing factories.

The Depression etched itself on the faces, habits and minds of those who endured it; the cautious, thrifty behaviour of this generation often a source of amusement to the next one. 'Don't throw that away, son, you never know when it might come in handy.'

Their homes and garden sheds overflow with 'come in handies'. These squirrel habits and a reluctance to be in any kind of debt are the abiding signs of the survivors, the marks of those who absorbed those painful lessons of the 1930s.

Historian Geoffrey Bolton points out that Australians still talk more about the Depression than many other nations.

I often have it said to me by people outside Australia that they're surprised by the scar which this seems to have left on the national consciousness. They say other places had depressions which were just as bad in the early 1930s, but we didn't make such a big thing of it as the Australians.

And I think we do partly because the normal expectation of Australians is that Australia is a place where we're going to prosper and do a bit better for ourselves. People become outraged that the dream is not going to become reality, and they regard this as a bit of abnormality, something outside the normal

No bathroom.

course of nature, that shouldn't be allowed to happen.

Allowed to happen or not, some must have wondered if it would ever end. Perhaps writer Donald Stuart summed up the feelings of many of the young of his time:

> It did last a long time when you consider that a lad of, say, fifteen, he was twenty before there was any great daylight. The morning star might come up but it was a hell of a long time before sunrise.

(Based on the ABC Radio documentary broadcast in October 1983)

The home struggle, 1935.

Moore River Settlement, 1948.

OUT OF SIGHT, OUT OF MIND
Aboriginal Internment

When I first arrived at the Mogumber siding I thought that was where the Mission would be but instead of that there was about eight miles through sandplain country, with not a thing in sight. I felt it was terribly isolated. It was out of sight, out of mind.

      Sister Eileen Heath, Anglican Deaconess, 1935.

It looked like they didn't want them to mingle with the white people. They got them in one little heap. When a family came here they got as far as the compound where we are sitting now and that was like, to me it was like a drafting yard. The lambs were kept in and the mums and dads were sent down to the camp.

      The late Ned Mippey, former inmate of Moore River.

In September 1985, Ned Mippey and I were sitting on a pleasant slope overlooking the Moore River, some one hundred and fifty kilometres north of Perth. We were beginning a vivid interview for a radio documentary which I would call 'Out Of Sight Out Of Mind'.

I was getting my bearings, in every sense, about Moore River. I'd heard so many stories about this place and what it had meant to the hundreds of people who had been sent to the Moore River Native Settlement between 1917 and 1951. The settlement is also known as Mogumber, the railway halt some twelve kilometres distant, where Aboriginal people bound for Moore River were consigned.

This sunny stretch of countryside, its tree-hidden river trickling into deep pools below the bright green banks where we sat, seemed to reflect nothing of the poignant stories I'd been told by both European and Aboriginal witnesses to the history of Moore River Settlement. The air was alive with insects and bird calls, and fresh with the warm scent of pines and peppermint gum.

Ned Mippey, who died early in 1992, is greatly missed in his community. He had lived, with his family for many years, at Moora, some forty kilometres north of Mogumber, where he spent his later years teaching the Nyungar language and culture to his community. In 1985 he accompanied me on a journey back to Moore River and helped me see the settlement through Aboriginal eyes.

Ned knew much, not just about Moore River, but about the resources of the country, and the ancient and recent history of his people.

We'd met two years earlier. I'd been recording material for a documentary about the Aboriginal experience of the twentieth century in Australia: 'Anybody Could Afford Us', the subject of an earlier chapter of this book. He'd told me stories then which convinced me of the significance of Moore River to both the Aboriginal and European history of this century.

Together we mapped out the Moore River site again. Ned pointed out important features, the chapel, kitchen and superintendent's

At Moore River Settlement, 1948.

house and garden. The few buildings that remain dominate the high ground above the river.

There's almost no sign of the former superintendent's residence and many of the outbuildings are slowly falling inwards in a tangle of creepers and saplings, reclaimed by the bush they once usurped.

Moore River is really two settlements in one. On the high ground, well above the river, the dormitories and chapel for the children who boarded there still stand.

They now serve the present owners, the Budjarra Aboriginal Community. Below them the compound for the older people straggled down the slopes towards the river. Little trace remains of its lean-to buildings and rough enclosures. 'There's the boob!' Ned was pointing to a dingy adobe building, if you could call it a building, down the hill from where we stood. 'That's where you went if the superintendent sent you.'

We entered through a narrow passage. To the left there was a dark, damp and windowless room. The 'boob' was designed as a temporary detention centre for offenders.

> *You'd fry in the summer and freeze in the winter. But that's where you got put if you were seen even talking to the girls. Some of the girls used to run away too. They ended up in here, maybe for two days at a time.*

Moore River wasn't the only government native settlement in Western Australia. Both black and partly black children and adults were frequently sent to various government settlements such as Carolup in the Great Southern district. But Moore River was the most notorious. Aboriginal leader Robert Bropho describes it as a place where

> *Aboriginal people were congregated to live as whole family units and groups of people. A settlement where Aboriginal people were herded up and where they had to live.*

Arnold Franks, from the Murchison district, ended his childhood at Moore River.

> *My mother got tooken away when I was a little fellow, and married. She couldn't take me with her. This was the part that really hurt me. I was a Native Affairs child born on a reserve so therefore, I'm under the government.*
>
> *The children that didn't have fathers were tooken away from up the North. My mother came from the Murchison country see. When they got there them days, Wongai, Wonamullas, Yamagis, you name 'em, they brought 'em in from all over. Now a lot of these fellows couldn't talk English. And the superintendent'd have a book in his hand, and he'd have the black tracker standing alongside of him, who didn't understand reading or writing or even couldn't count. And they'd walk along the line and they say to a bloke, 'What's your name?' One fellow, he can't talk, he'll say, 'Waiadero'. They don't understand his name. They'll put him down as 'Friday'. 'What this fellow name?'*
>
> *'Oh he can't talk English', or he say something in Australian language (that's Aborigine language, that's proper Australian language) they'll call him 'Wheelbarrow!' 'Next one? Put him down as "Fifty"!' and so on, 'Horseshoe', 'Tommy', 'Penny' or 'Billycan Bill'!*

Aboriginal people, young and old, lost their names, families and homes, often, as Bella Yappo recalls, without explanation.

> *They used to bring a lot of people away from where they lived. There was girls there from Derby, even old women. They used to bring them down, for some unknown reason. I don't know why. I have no idea why they done it. I couldn't say from that day to this.*

Boys and girls were at Moore River because that was where the

Government decreed they should spend their childhood and teenage years. It was where you were sent to be 'out of sight, out of mind'.

Playwright and poet Jack Davis knew at first-hand the effect of this policy in the 1940s.

> You were policed by black policemen, black trackers. You were locked up in the compound at six o'clock and you were let out at six o'clock in the morning. You had to go out to work. You weren't paid for your labour, though labour was really not the hard work. I can't say that about our masters. We were stood over, but it was this policing you all your time, all your patterns of behaviour. If you had a sore on your arm, someone would grab you, somebody in authority, pull your hand up, 'You get up to the hospital! Go on!' So you went up to the hospital and they dressed it. They were looking after you but you had no independence.

Bella Yappo experienced the same monotonous regimen.

> We worked. When the bell rang you had to toe the line and be there. We had a big kitchen where everybody went for their meals, the dining room. I worked in there too.

When Moore River fell into neglect during the Depression, Aboriginal children fared worse than their white counterparts. Arnold Franks can still remember the hungry 1930s.

> We got one meal a day, greasy stew. What was left over from the trotters and the guts, and they boiled this all up with a onion and potato. They had a big copper for a boiler, boil the stew. Now you got that meal with a slice of bread and fat. If you were lucky enough you pinch another slice, and put it down your shirt. Now that meal got to last you all day. Now you got to go down the river, we had a river in the settlement where we

The compound police, c1917.

catch gilgies and little fish (long tail they call them), little yabbies, all them sort of things. We ate what crawled, even bobtail goanna, bee'ive bird, little birds. We ate every bird, every fish, that crawled, walked, or flied, or swim. We had to eat to get our tucker.

Bella Yappo is sure that many girls escaped from Moore River, not with any hope of getting away for ever, but because anything was better than being cooped up.

A lot of them used to run away. They used to run away and come up to Moora or go out to Walebing, because there was a lot of people out at Walebing, at the reserve. They used to fetch them back and lock them up, but they'd do it again. They used to be the ones that couldn't settle or just wanted to get out and see what life was all about, I suppose.

Moore River was set up in 1917 by the State Government as a training centre for young Aboriginal and part-Aboriginal people. The idea was to give the boys skills in station or farm work and the girls domestic training. It was an obvious way of preparing them for work in a white world. Jack Davis, who took Moore River for the setting of his play *No Sugar*, was himself sent there for training.

For a few years it worked very well. Then we had the Depression of the 1930s in which it really deteriorated because finance was cut back. In fact, I think you could keep an Aboriginal person in Moore River for two and six per week whereas they used to pay six shillings a week to keep a prisoner in Fremantle prison. So not much money was spent on Moore River at the time.
And then of course Moore River deteriorated to such an extent that it was a home for murderers, thieves and God knows what! People who had been speared came in here. Old people who came in here to die. It became a clearing house for Aboriginal people, a clearing house in the sense that they were

Kitchen at Moore River Settlement, 1949.

sent there just to stay there and decay away in mind, body and soul. And that was what Moore River was about!

Ned Mippey, whose childhood was spent at Moore River, with his family, later found work as an apprentice carpenter in nearby Moora. By this time he had lost touch with his mother, who had returned to domestic work at the settlement.

> I had me mother to think of. And she finished going back to the Mogumber Mission to look after the girls in the dormitory, and I was working with Jim Ash when she passed away. I was a carpenter. We was making coffins and all that.
> He said to me, 'You'd better go up there and measure Clara Leyland'. I said, 'Hey, that's my mother!' See, that's how, you didn't know. You was away from them. Well, I just stopped. I looked at him and he said, 'Well, Ned, you'd better go home. Go back down to the camp.'

Moore River symbolised the European approach to 'The Aboriginal Question' in the first half of this century.

Increased European settlement, especially after 1870, when the North-west began to open up, meant that pastoralists and farmers displaced the traditional Aboriginal people from their ancient hunting and watering grounds, their 'increase places'.

Those Aborigines who stayed on in their own country did so on European terms, doing white people's work and eating white people's food. In lieu of payment for their services men became stockmen or farm workers, and women cooks or maids.

In isolated areas Aboriginal women played another role. Given the frequent absence of white females, local Aboriginal women became de facto wives and, inevitably, mothers of part-European, part-Aboriginal children, infants who were sometimes, though not always, an embarrassment to their natural fathers, the pastoralist or his station manager.

But if the father wasn't embarrassed, the government certainly was. Some fathers were well known to, if not themselves members of, the Legislative Council.

This small conservative group dominated the colonial government of Western Australia in the nineteenth century. Its power base was the land, and its labour force, especially in the north, the Aboriginal population.

That workforce, created mainly through the enforced recruitment of Aboriginal labour, and partly through white sexual need, created a new kind of Aborigine, a person caught between two worlds: traditional Aboriginal society, and station life where colour and status condemned them to menial work.

Traditional Aboriginal society was now in decline in almost every sense of the word. Although Aborigines were not, as often stated by government officials, 'a dying race', the nature of the race was changing. Aborigines of mixed origin were growing in number, a highly visible reminder to Europeans of their own contribution to the so-called 'Aboriginal problem'.

Bruce McClarty, former Deputy Commissioner for Native Welfare, pointed out that by the 1930s,

> *In the more densely settled white areas of the State, the Aboriginal population, far from dying out, was on the increase. And this increase was generated mainly not by miscegenation between white settlers and Aboriginal women but by propagation of the caste people among themselves. And there was a very rapid growth in the size of Aboriginal families.*
>
> *So that on the one hand you had a sort of conscience-stricken effort to prove to the world that we weren't using them as slaves, that we weren't sort of deliberately killing them off, that we were trying our best to make life easier for them and a bit more tenable for them, but at the same time diminishing the nuisance that they constituted to the white population.*

But if Aboriginal people, and especially part-Aboriginal people, were going to continue to provide a living reproach to Europeans, they had to be assimilated quietly and efficiently. It was the only way of diminishing the 'nuisance'.

Hence the Moore River training scheme. From now on there would be no troublesome questions about ownership of land or the conditions of employment for Aborigines. Moore River would enable them to take their place in European society at an appropriate level. They would be supervised by European staff, taught Christian virtues and given elementary schooling. The end product would be a docile, well-disciplined, semi-skilled pool of labour for Western Australian homes and farms.

Moore River was run by a succession of superintendents, some from a military background, with little or no knowledge of Aboriginal society. Irene Turner, who worked briefly as a nurse at the settlement in 1940, was barked at for 'not walking three paces ahead of the natives'. The superintendent was assisted in the maintenance of discipline by 'black trackers', whose skills were much in demand when inmates ran away.

There was a hospital, staffed by a matron and a succession of inexperienced, but often dedicated, kindly nursing staff who managed as best they could with inadequate supplies and equipment.

The school was staffed by government teachers and was under the control of the State Education Department. But, like the hospital, it was poorly resourced and the Aboriginal pupils were not encouraged to progress beyond basic literacy.

Moore River Native Settlement was not just an attempt to grapple with 'the Aboriginal problem', it was also designed to remove it from the public gaze. The site could hardly have been chosen with more care. Anglican Deaconess Sister Eileen Heath came to work at Moore River in 1935.

> When I first arrived at the Mogumber siding I thought that was where the Mission would be but instead of that there was about eight miles through sandplain country, with not a thing in sight. I felt it was terribly isolated. It was 'out of sight, out of mind'.

Kindergarten playpen at Moore River Settlement, 1949.

'Sister Eileen, she was real good to us!' is a tribute still paid to her by many Moore River inmates. Arnold Franks knew, as a kid, that Sister Eileen spent her own money taking a group of children down to Cottesloe for a week's holiday.

Sister Eileen still works for the Anglican Church in Alice Springs and was willing enough to help with information on Moore River when I called to see her there. It isn't the first time she has given testimony about the settlement.

In 1944 she wrote a report for the Anglican Church which was highly critical of the lack of education, incentives for young people, and the physical conditions at Moore River.

It did not win her many friends, especially in the State Government bureaucracy. Forty years on, her criticism was just as trenchant.

> *The sanitation in the dormitories was absolutely appalling. The staff, when they went in, would say, I'll have to have a cigarette before I go in! The children had to be locked in at night time for safety and protection. Once locked in there was no supervision whatever. There were no toilets, just sanitary buckets which were emptied each morning. The dormitories were very dimly lit, cyclone beds, no sheets of course. Blankets, bug-ridden!*
>
> *When anybody special was coming to the settlement we had a stock of sheets which were put on the beds especially so that if anybody wanted to go into the dormitories they got the impression that the children always had sheets on their beds.*
>
> *The compound was lined with pine trees or fir trees, and when anybody special was coming they were whitewashed all the way up the trunks.*

Even before Moore River was set up, the means to bring Aboriginal people into one place already existed. The Aboriginal Protection Act of 1905 allowed Aboriginal children to be forcibly removed from their parents by the police. Although this removal was said 'to be in the children's best interests', in reality it meant

Girls dormitory, Moore River Settlement, 1949.

removing unwanted 'half-caste' offspring from station reserves, and from homes where white men lived with de facto Aboriginal wives.

Alice Nannup was to experience the effect of this policy and her story vividly illustrates the situation for many Aboriginal or part-Aboriginal children in the 1920s and 1930s.

Alice was born in 1912 in the Roebourne district of the Northwest. Her father was a European station owner, and her mother a local Aborigine.

Her childhood was happy enough. Her father once bawled her out for speaking in her mother's language but otherwise Alice can recall only his affection for her. There was only one threat to her childhood security, the fear that she could be taken away.

> The Aboriginal Affairs used to come round North, scouting for little kids to take them away from their parents. When they knew they were around, my mother and whoever else was there, they used to make sandwiches up and give it to us and we'd have to stay in the quarters all day and if the people came walking around we'd get under the bed and hide so they wouldn't take us away.

That threat became much more real when her parents separated and Alice went to live with her mother at the Roebourne reserve.

As a result of presumably good intentions on the part of neighbours of her father, the Campbells, Alice was to spend the rest of her childhood in Moore River.

The Campbells, who were about to retire from station life, took Alice out of the reserve and into their own home. There she did household chores with two other girls. When the Campbells went south they took all three girls with them, having promised Alice's father that they would ensure her education.

The voyage south was not a promising start.

> We came down on the Mindaroo and on that boat I was sick all the way down. The boat had a sort of balcony, whatever you

call it, and we used to sit out there. They never took us into the dining room. We sat out there and, of course, we used to talk in our own lingo those times and we'd cry for home. We'd say, 'Oh! If only we could just go back home and be with our mother!' You know, it used to be heartbreaking.

The Campbells took Alice to Perth to attend an interview with the Chief Protector of Aborigines, Mr A O Neville. Neville controlled the movements and activities of all Aboriginal people in the State. He was also the administrator who had set up the Moore River Native Settlement in 1917.

Alice was sent outside while the Campbells discussed her future with the Chief Protector. Afterwards she learned that she was to go to Moore River for her care and education. The year was 1925.

The train was a bit late that night and when we got to Mogumber we were just taken into the dormitory. Everybody else was in bed. We woke up in the morning to find little black faces all over the place. I'd never seen anything like it in my life. I was so worried and upset. Some of them were friendly. Some of them were hostile.

Some of them wanted to fight us but we just picked out a few friends. First thing they asked you, 'Where 'd'you come from?' And if you say 'North', the Nor'west girls'd take you under their wings and the Sou'westers'd stick on one side and the Nor'westers on the other.

Alice's education ended at grade three. After that she went into the Moore River sewing room to make clothes for the Forrest River Mission and other places. She was paid in chocolates and not in cash. Not, as she admits, that she minded at the time. But to this day she still feels bitter that she was denied any effective schooling.

They didn't want to give us a real education. Mr Neville said one day, he said, 'As long as they can count money and write their name, that's all they need'. What sort of education is that?

When Alice, aged sixteen, finally left Mogumber it was to go into domestic service in the country, working in police stations and on farms.

She never saw her parents again. Her mother died five years after Alice had been taken south. But Alice only learnt of her death much later on, when she herself was married with children of her own.

Alice remembers her father's repeated but unsuccessful attempts to visit her at Moore River, visits always blocked by the authorities. She could receive his generous presents, have his letters read to her, but he was not permitted to come and see her. She was told, 'It's better that way'. No reason was given.

After a while the letters stopped coming and Alice heard no more. Years later she was to learn from a Geraldton friend that her father had been surprised in his tent one night, possibly on one of his trips south, robbed and killed. 'And in his will he left me four hundred pounds. And I never even received that.'

It took Alice forty-two years to find her other relatives, an aunt and an uncle in Roebourne. They hadn't heard of her in all that time.

> My mother's sister was the only living auntie I had. I went there one morning at half-past seven. They were getting breakfast ready. I went to the door and knocked and said, 'Do you know who I am?' And they said, 'No, we don't'. And I just laughed and Uncle Bill said, 'It's not Alice is it?' And I said, 'That's me!' Well, look the game was on. There were tears and laughter and everything, you know, they couldn't believe it because I was only a little girl when I left home.

Alice has also described her life as a domestic servant after she left Moore River, experiences which featured in a radio programme, 'Alice Nannup; Her Early Life'. And her full life story

Internees, 1948.

appears in her own book, *When the Pelican Laughed*.

While home for a while, Moore River was also the gateway to an uncertain future, as Ned Mippey was to discover.

> *We were put there and we had to stay there, until such time when we left. When they said we were going on. That hurt a bit too, by going away. I was leaving me friends and that's more or less something. That's out into the wilderness.*

Aboriginal people of all ages and from all over Western Australia were sent to, and lived out much of their lives at, Moore River.

The law encouraged the removal of children from their parents. But why were adults from the far North in exile from their own lands? Again the answer lies in legislation. When Jack Davis was a boy, all Aboriginal people were

> *wards of the State and that was the law. A magistrate only had to sign a piece of paper and say, 'You're going to Moore River!,' and people would be sent there accordingly. And hundreds of people were uprooted like this and sent there. And of course this not only happened in the South. It happened all over Western Australia.*

He still remembers one remarkable couple.

> *Well, I always have very strong, very vivid memories of an old man who was called Skipper. Of course being a boy of fourteen anybody who had a long white beard was old, but looking back I think he would have been about fifty years of age. His wife was blind, an enormously big woman. Her name was Nora. She was completely blind and he was I would have said about eighty per cent blind and they lived together. And one of the most vivid experiences of my life was to sit down at night and hear those two sing. I have never heard anything in my life since or before*

Moore River camp, c1917.

> that could rival those two in power of voice. Everybody in the whole community used to stop when these two used to sing their Aboriginal songs at the top of their voice, the power and the range and the tremolo. It was just absolutely amazing; it was marvellous.
>
> They were singing about their country which they knew they were never going to see again. It was all they were singing about, their country, which was the Kimberleys.

Much of the forced removal to Moore River occurred during the tenure of A O Neville, who was Chief Protector of Aborigines from 1916 to 1940.

To be fair to Neville, he did not always condone the practice. He was well aware that Moore River was used as a dumping ground by local authorities when they wanted to get rid of Aborigines around their towns. But Neville, apparently, could do little about it. The Moore River Native Settlement had been abused in this way almost from its inception during World War One. At that time Neville was in charge of northern agricultural development and had temporarily lost control of his responsibilities for Aboriginal people in the southern half of the State. When he resumed his role as Chief Protector, in 1922, it was with a reduced budget and very little bargaining power.

Neville retired in 1940. But many a Moore River inmate outstayed him, casualties of the policies of forced removal and dumping. When Stanley Middleton became Commissioner for Native Welfare in 1946, he resolved to pay an early visit to the settlement.

> And my first recollection of Moore River ever since has been that I could smell it half a mile away before I got there, the very strong, almost overpowering smell of creosote mixed with human odours and so on. And the second impression it left on me was the attitude of the inmates. These people just sat there absolutely silent and just stared and it was almost unreal.
>
> It affected me rather profoundly because it was so obvious

TREATMENT OF ABORIGINES.

MISSIONARIES' ALLEGATIONS

Melbourne, Jan. 12.

Addressing students at the Australian Board of Missions' Summer School, at Frankston, the Rev. Mr. J. S. Needham, chairman of the Australian Board of Missions, said that more than 80 per cent. of aboriginal girls sent out in to the world came back to the missions degraded by white men. Throughout Australia white people raised objections whenever an aborigine tried to earn his own living. In Western Australia a protest against the selling of sleepers by the blacks was made to the Government, and at Cairns action was taken to prevent them selling fish. The aim of the missions was to enable the blacks to earn their own livings on mission stations. If only those interested in the work were more interested and more money was available, much could be done.

Miss Lily Newman, a missionary at the Moore River aborigine settlement at Mogumber, Western Australia, said that work among the young aboriginal women was disheartening. They were trained as domestic helps and sent out into the world, but many of them returned to the station expectant mothers or very badly treated. Some employers, because the girls were black, made them eat their meals from old tin plates placed on the doorsteps outside the houses.

Miss Newman added that another great problem was gambling. The men went away to work and returned to camp and played two up. She also said that some of the half-castes at the mission station were Chinese or Japanese.

Report from the Kalgoorlie Miner, 15 January 1934.

> that they were a people who were psychologically very disturbed. It wasn't natural. There were no greetings, not even 'Gooday!' or anything, you know, not a word!

Stanley Middleton was also grimly aware that the pre-war habits had not been broken.

> As far as the government was concerned, it was a convenient dumping ground for unwanted natives. Take Northam, for example, one of the nearest large towns. If the Chairman of the Road Board, as it was then, felt that there were too many natives there, than were required for their purposes, like the off-season between harvesting and seeding, they would get the police. They didn't have to get the Department's approval. The police would simply round them up and take them into Moore River, out of sight and out of mind. In many cases they were kept there for so long they couldn't remember on what grounds they were originally sent there.

Bob Bropho, of the Swan River fringe dwellers community, spent part of his teenage years at Moore River.

> Moore River was like a holding pen for Aboriginal people, coming from country areas that was troublesome, through the police and the courts they would be sentenced there for a time period of six months or whatever.

Some of those country areas were remote in the extreme, often districts where Aboriginal and European society scarcely interacted, except to clash over land use.

Margaret Morgan is the daughter of missionary Roy Schenk who served at the Mount Margaret Mission in the North-eastern Goldfields in the years before World War Two. It was from nearby Laverton that in 1926 the police sent fourteen people down to Moore River, a thousand kilometres west of their own country.

Mission Group, c1930.

Although Margaret's father regarded the deportees as within his care, he was powerless to prevent their removal.

> *He didn't know then. All he saw was that when he went down to the train he saw this cattle truck with the little notice, 'Fifteen Niggers for Mogumber'.*

Alice Nannup knows the story of the Mount Margaret people from the Mogumber end. It became part of the folklore of Moore River.

> *There was a blind man. There were women and children. They were very shy, couldn't speak English some of them! They just lived on the compound, and every now and again they'd move camp, just kept on moving camp. Each night they'd move to another place. And one night they made the escape and went back home.*

The thousand kilometre journey back to Mount Margaret Mission was to take less than fourteen days. The group moved by night to avoid detection and steered by the stars. They had to leave the blind man behind in a paddock but he bawled for help. A kindly farmer picked him up, helped him trace his people and get home. Another, an old man, had to be left behind, sitting by the camp fire. Most, however, got back to their own community.

Reggie Johnston, who still lives in the Laverton area, saw the homecoming.

> *They was glad when they went back. But some of the old people died when they returned, but many of them half-castes never returned.*

The Mount Margaret escape seems to have been the biggest breakout in the history of Moore River, but bolder spirits, especially

A O Neville at Mount Margaret Mission, 1931.

among the young, continued to run away from Mogumber for the next thirty years.

Sister Eileen knew only too well what happened to girls who ran away.

> They were tracked by the trackers, apprehended and brought back again and locked up in a place that was called 'the boob', which was a small galvanised iron building with no proper facilities either for washing or for toilet.

Commissioner Stanley Middleton made his first visit to Moore River in 1946. The boob was still in use.

> And one of the buildings was introduced to me by the superintendent as being 'the boob' and I knew, because I'm a country Queenslander, what was meant by 'boob'. It's prison! And I said, 'What have you got this for?'
> 'Oh!' he said, 'we lock them up!'
> 'Why?' I said. 'Oh!' he said, 'if they do anything wrong, you know, fight or do anything they shouldn't, we put them in here for the night'.
> 'But', I said, 'on what authority?'
> 'Oh!' he said, 'I'm the superintendent!' There were barred windows. Now that was another thing that shocked me, it was so illegal.

Moore River shocked Commissioner Middleton sufficiently for him to close it down as a State-run institution in 1950. The settlement was handed over to the Methodist Church which ran it as the Mogumber mission, opening in 1951. The subsequent history of Moore River was much happier.

Paradoxically, Moore River was not entirely negative in its effect on Aboriginal society. Talk long enough to people who went there and you begin to notice an ambivalence in their comments on the place.

Sports day at Moore River Settlement, c1948

There are bad memories of poor food, lack of education and sheer frustration at the meaninglessness of life. But there are also memories of childhood friendships, of defying authority and getting away with it and of perverse pride in having endured the place.

For those children taken from their parents, Moore River was 'home', the only place they really knew. For years many came back from time to time, sometimes just to see staff who were good to them (mention Sister Eileen and you're guaranteed a warm Aboriginal smile any time). And some will still cheerfully admit to coming back 'just to sit on the banks above the river and look at the old place again.'

But there was another legacy, unintended by its founders. Moore River was at its worst a concentration camp. At its best it was a university of adversity, a centre where Aboriginal people from many different parts of the State met and found common cause. By concentrating a diverse population in one place, some elements of Aboriginality were kept alive.

As Jack Davis observed, 'It made some of us very weak. And it made some of us very strong'.

Moore River is a painful chapter in our history. Jack Davis sums it up:

> *I think everybody was completely ignorant of how to handle it. Aboriginal people didn't know how to handle it. Certainly the government didn't know how to handle it. They were suddenly stuck with a race of people who were here and was not supposed to be here. The attempt at keeping full-blood people down had failed and all of a sudden the half-caste population was there on their doorstep and most of them were related to them, and they didn't know how to handle it.*

(Based on the ABC Radio documentary broadcast in April 1986)

Swimming in Moore River, 1948.

Karri forest, near Bridgetown.

SOMETHING UNIQUE, SOMETHING MAJESTIC
Life in the Forests

I feel that there's something unique, something majestic about them. I feel that they're not really appreciated as they should be.

> Olive Robinson, long-time resident of the timber town of Manjimup.

The tall karri appear just south of that town on the South Coast Highway.

I like the country all the way down the road from Perth to the far South-west of Western Australia; the flat but pleasant pastures of the Harvey dairy district, the backdrop of the Darling Ranges, the fertile orchard country around Donnybrook, the broad valleys and rolling hills of Balingup and Bridgetown, always attractive, whether in their burnt summer hues or in the cool green of spring or winter.

The road climbs out of yet one more pleasant valley, across a high plateau, and leads into Manjimup, a fruit growing and timber industry centre. But nothing along that two hundred kilometre drive prepares the traveller for the first sight of the karri forest. The open landscape changes suddenly. A few kilometres south of Manjimup you enter a silent, mysterious landscape, a world of graceful, tall trees: the karri.

> *The karri tree and the karri forest, it's one of the most beautiful trees in the world, and the forest itself, particularly the primeval forest, what we call the virgin forest, it had a cathedral-like structure, somewhere where you feel entirely relaxed and the kind of place you would always want to come back to. That's the way it affects me.*

Jack Thomson, now in his eighties, still feels that way about the forest. He has spent much of a working lifetime amongst timber, first as an apprentice faller and later as a forester with the Forestry Department.

That's the way it affects me too when I drive into the karri country. I slow down, peer through the top half of the windscreen to see the crowns of the karri as they tower on either side of the road, and wind the window open to take in the sharp, feral scent of the karri wattle, the ferny shrub that surrounds the huge trunks of the karri.

There's scarcely a house, a cow or any sign of settlement as you travel south; nothing, it seems, but the huge ivory-pink pillars of the

Bush railway, near Pemberton.

karri and their luxuriant undergrowth.

But there is a human world inside that forest, a scattering of small mill towns, many of them shrinking today and some, like Shannon Mill, gone for ever, the wooden homes carted elsewhere to make holiday houses for escapees from the city. The bush is already closing in on former streets and gardens. It is as though the town had never been.

The timber business of the 1990s is a world apart from places like Shannon Mill. Today timber mills are centralised and mechanised and the forest workforce far smaller and specialised.

But if you read Katharine Susannah Prichard's novel *Working Bullocks*, published in 1926, you re-enter that vanished world, a forest crisscrossed by bullock and horse tracks, of scattered forest camps where the fallers lived, of small mill towns that were home to hundreds of families in the years before World War Two, a forest that rang to sounds no louder than an axe or a bullocky's curse, a world without chainsaws, prime movers, clear felling and a woodchip industry.

Jack Thomson worked in the South-west during that era. Affectionately known throughout the West as 'Man of the Trees', Jack is respected for his fearless championship of conservation values and his outspoken criticism of many modern forestry methods, views which do not always endear him to men who see forests solely as a source of profit.

Jack left school at fourteen and worked as an apprentice with the Forestry Department in Manjimup, planting out seedling trees to replace timber taken from the forest. The work was hard and the hours were long. Jack started each day at first light and toiled till five in the afternoon, with a Saturday shift included. A forty-eight hour week. And this was manual labour, with crosscut saws, axes and expert felling by hand and eye.

> *You just couldn't tear in and fell a tree anywhere. A tree marker had to be an experienced faller himself and he would carefully note where the tree's natural lean was, but if he decided, no, it*

Fellers using a crosscut saw.

can't go out there, where it would naturally go, but I can swing it into that opening there, he'd mark it there. The faller'd have to go to a bit more trouble to lift it and throw it over in that direction, so that there'd be minimum damage to the remaining stand of timber.

But tree felling wasn't just difficult, it could also be dangerous. Retired faller Charlie Tozer saw plenty of the hazards in his long working life.

Well, you never learnt felling unless you got with an experienced man. And that was the set-up. If anybody got killed or left, well then you was taken out of the gang. If you had your name down for a job falling, and you took his place.

Danger was not confined to the felling of trees. Logs could still kill when they reached the timber mill. Mill worker Maurice Battilana saw several accidents on the bench as big timber went through.

It was dangerous work, really dangerous. Because those days they never had a guard at the tail of the saw. I've seen one chap killed and I've seen another, his leg broken on a rip bench, when they were finishing off and the half-timber broke and came down and broke his leg. It was a slaughterhouse. To be honest I'd hate to have one of my own kids go work in a mill.

Kathleen Ffoulkes's father was the victim of a mill accident. When an incorrectly knotted rope gave way in the elevator at Dean Mill, he fell four metres, broke his wrist, arm and thigh and spent twelve months in hospital.

Kathleen Ffoulkes also knew of others, unluckier than her father, who met their deaths in the big timber, not through carelessness with axe and saw, but from hazards inherent in the forest itself.

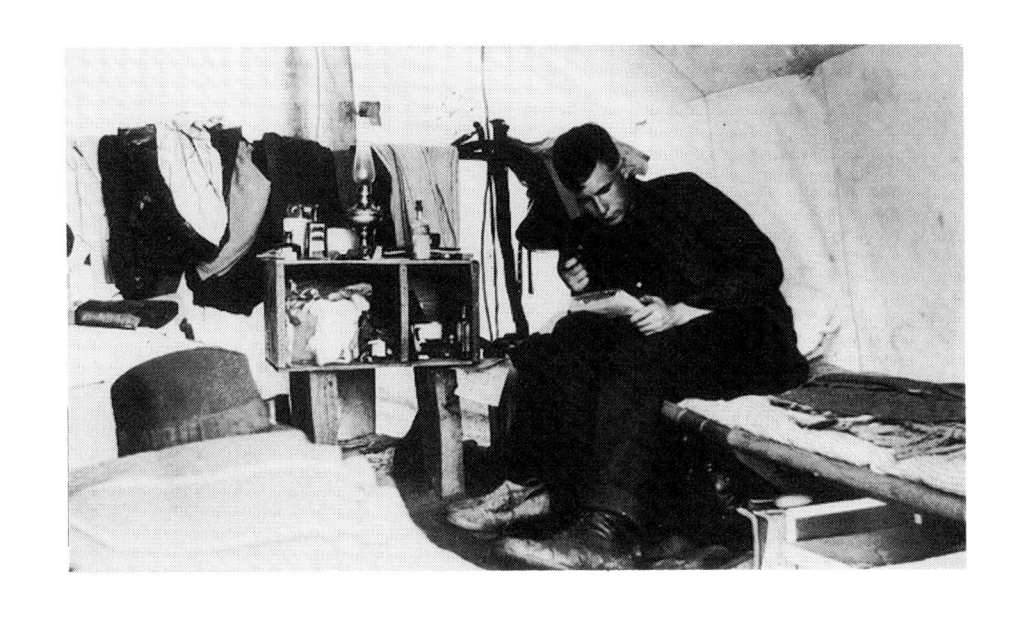

Forestry school tent, 1923.

> They have what they call in the bush widow-makers. And they are dead branches that are in trees and if a wind becomes high, they drop on men's heads and there's been lots of people – their husbands have died through widow-makers.

Jack Thomson knew one of those victims well.

> I went out to see a faller out west of Manjimup. And the last tree he was to fall that night, there was a hanger from another tree hanging over his head and he was worrying about this damn thing all night, y'know, hoping that no one would walk underneath it. And he went out next morning and the main limb came down and killed him as dead as a doornail.

Dangers apart, the bush life, for many forest workers, meant long periods of isolation from families or the settled forest communities in the mill towns. While some men lived and worked together in the bush timber camps, others were pieceworkers, cutting marked trees on their own. Former forester Ron Meldrum did this sort of work for many years.

> For the most part you'd be camped out some miles from the towns, in a tent, and you worked no particular hours. You found your own way out to the workplace. And you found your own way home, and probably carried food supplies for the week in some cases.

Given Jack Thomson's experience of timber camp meals, many timber workers would have been glad of their own provisions.

> The cook's chief equipment was a good strainer and plenty of vinegar because when the meat's half stinking and you pour plenty of vinegar over it, it takes the smell away. This is what we lived on. For breakfast you'd have bacon. I never ate a bit of bacon for twenty years after I left, salt as billy-oh! You know!

Cutting the trunk of a karri for transport to the mill.

> You'd start off the day spitting chips, thirsty as anything and even though you were in the South-west, you'd go three miles and not get a running creek in the summertime.

And those South-west winters could be cold. Faller Charlie Tozer kept warm working with axe and saw.

> You couldn't wear much clothes, very little clothes, just two flannel shirts, one tucked inside and the other hanging outside – that was a good protection against the weather or anything.

Today's foresters in four-wheel drives, parkas and hard hats might find it hard to relate to Charlie Tozer and Jack Thomson's 'all in a day's work' descriptions. Jack walked to work each day whatever the season.

> We used to go into the jarrah country. We used to get pretty wet there too but the rain – it's not all that bad. It falls in lumps, more or less.
>
> I remember once, the first camp I went on. We were camped on the Wilgaru – Balingup road, on the Balingup Brook, and we couldn't find a place to cross this brook, it was in flood, y'know, I suppose about thirty feet across and waist deep. And every morning (most of our work was on the other side) we had to lift up our ... every man cut his own crib, you had your own crib rolled up in a bit of newspaper and put in a handkerchief and you hung it on the back of your belt, with a jam tin billycan, tea and sugar. So we'd lift this up and just wade through this icy-cold water up to your waist. But after you'd walked for about half a mile you'd walked yourself warm again. You took that all in your stride!

The closest I came to experiencing Jack and Charlie's working conditions, and it was luxurious by comparison, was the cold wet

Hauling timber using a whim, c1920.

weekend that ABC *Folk and Beyond* presenter, Murray Jennings, and I spent, together with Bob Rummery, Alan Mann and other members of the West Australian Bush Orchestra, at Jardee mill just south of Manjimup.

We had borrowed the old Jardee schoolroom to record songs about the karri and the jarrah and the men who worked them, songs that I was later to weave into the radio feature on forest life. With technical producers Peter Burnett and Graham Boyd we carted a stereo mixer and umpteen microphones into the bush to get the right background, and to the accompaniment of melancholy magpies and dripping rain, taped a dozen bush songs.

Most of the melodies and the lyrics were written by Bob Rummery and Alan Mann, but two came from locals, Dawn Brittain and Bob Radojkovic, the latter a champion axeman as well as folk singer.

Dawn performed a haunting number, 'The Whim Track', a tender lament for the vanished people and ways of the forest. It ends with the death of an old bullocky.

> *They found him there in the morning.*
> *His story well told on his face.*
> *The spirits that haunt the old whim track*
> *had gathered the last of his race.*

Bob Radojkovic's song, 'Traces and Chains' also mourns the passing from the forest of the bullocky, his whim (an arched, two-wheeled log hauler), his animals and his way of life.

> *No more the sound of his stockwhip.*
> *His team from the valley has gone.*
> *The crosscut and axe are now silent.*
> *But the legend will live on and on.*
>
> *As he watches the smoke from his camp fire,*
> *drift with the soft morning breeze.*

> *The billy would sit quietly boiling*
> *in his world of bullocks and trees.*
>
> *His day it begins before sunrise.*
> *As he sets out the traces and chains.*
> *From the hot dusty days in December*
> *to the cold, ravaging, winter rains.*
>
> *Now the whim tracks have finally grown over*
> *where karris were hauled by the team*
> *to the landings away in the gully,*
> *by the side of meandering streams.*
>
> *But I'm sure that I still hear his stockwhip*
> *as I wander beneath the pale moon.*
> *Then realise that I'm only dreaming*
> *of a lifestyle that ended too soon.*

Listening to those singers on that cold, wet July day, I thought, is this how legends begin? Do the songs get written after the event rather than during it? Bob and Dawn were both singing of a time long past but their urge to preserve the spirit of that way of life was what counted.

One of my favourite songs from the day's recording at Jardee was 'Down Under'.

And it meant just that. Dawn Brittain's husband, Tom, an axeman himself, took us out the day before the Jardee singfest to the old pitsawing sites, deep in the bush, and climbed into their deep trenches to make plain the meaning of 'down under'.

The pits are now almost overgrown but in one or two places the locals have kept them as they once were, steep slits in which two men cut timber, one above and his less fortunate mate below.

As the song puts it,

Mum, I'm sending you a few bob.
For I've found myself a job
It ain't no high position.
I am treated with derision.
For I'm sawing up the forest logs
Down Under.

While he stands upon each log,
I am crouching like a dog.
For a stingy crust we split
those brutes asunder.
Through thick and through thin,
through the swearing and the din,
I see a different world from here
Down Under.

For I'm down in the pit.
On my knees and off the bit.
And the boss above is fearful
of a blunder.

We pull the pit crosscut
through the jarrah and blackbutt.
And I'm the mug that does it from
Down Under.

(Lyric Alan Mann)

Pitsawing was the job nobody wanted. In winter it meant working long hours up to your knees in mud, while sawdust rained down into your eyes. In summer your sweat turned the sawdust into glue and the ants crawled up your legs. And it wasn't much better for the top sawyer. He had the heavy lifting to do.

All forest work was hard on sawyers, fallers and mill hands alike, and even harder and more dangerous for the animals that worked with the timbermen.

The late Leo Wheatley drove bullock teams in the Manjimup area from boyhood onwards. He had great affection for them and for the horse teams that also hauled the forest logs.

But he harboured no romantic illusions about the passing of working animals from the bush. He knew only too well the conditions they worked in.

> *I was very glad when tractors came in because it was a cruel thing to go into one of those horse yards and see the shocking state of the horses, great tears torn out in their shoulders and not only from the work they had to do.*

It wasn't just the work they had to do, it was also the way they were treated. Forester Ron Meldrum was also glad to see them go.

> *Oh, I don't think anybody regrets the passing of the bullock teams and the horse teams because of the terrific cruelty they suffered in that time. And not only from the nature of the work they had to do, the bullocks working in deep bog and in the summertime working in dust, breathing and sucking in dust, particularly the horse teams. Many horses have died, their lungs have been cut out by dust. And by inefficient and uncaring operators who fitted them with bad harness and didn't feed them and so forth. No, I don't think anybody could be sorry to see the passing of bullocks and horses.*

But even if they received humane treatment, animals lived a risky life, along with the foresters they served. Jack Thomson, a great lover of timber horses, was well aware of the natural hazards they faced working in the bush.

> *When they were towing a log for instance, often, a horse got speared in the belly with a green stick that had broken off a*

> limb. The horse in front of him steps on it and lifts it up and it runs into his belly.

I talked at length to Charlie Tozer about the partnership between animals and men in the forest. Today Charlie lives in Manjimup and cuts nothing taller than the roses in his garden. But the forest has been his life and his memory for detail is remarkable. Like Leo Wheatley, he has always admired the patient strength of the bullocks and the ease with which they hauled logs from the forest, working sometimes in teams of sixteen, using a whim.

> The whim was like a big arch on two wheels, with a pole. The pole was tipped up backwards and the arch hit the log. And then it was chained tight round. As the bullocks pulled, that would lift the log up in the air and off the ground.

The bullockies themselves, those characters celebrated in the poetry of Judith Wright and the novels of Katharine Susannah Prichard, are all gone, along with the bullocks they drove so hard. Charlie Tozer, when younger, held them in some awe.

> They were pretty tough old fellers. They never mucked around. If the bullocks wouldn't do what they wanted them to do, if the load, say, was a bit heavy, they'd get stuck into them with a whip or wave and shout, wave their arms and scream. Yeah, they could swear all right. Don't worry about that!

With the passing of the bullockies and the pitsaws, forestry entered the age of the motor truck and the mechanical saw. More recently the chainsaw and the articulated log hauler have changed the forest and the forester's life for ever.

Today a faller can cut down a two-hundred-year-old karri in ten minutes and, towed by a powerful truck, the stripped trunk can reach the mill inside an hour. The impact of this technology on

Bullock team near Pemberton, 1935.

both the environment and traditional employment of foresters is only too evident.

But in the pre-war period there was only steam power driving the mill saws, and steam locomotives hauled the logs in from the landings along the bush rail tracks, light railways operated by men like retired fireman and driver Roy Kelly.

Roy still lives in Pemberton and within sound of the mill his train fed with logs each day. But the whistles and snorts of the steam locos don't echo through the Pemberton valley any more. Like the pitsawyers and bullockies they have vanished from the forest.

But steam engines live on in the folklore, and perhaps with good reason, if there's any truth in Roy Kelly's theory about their effect on timber town population figures.

> *They reckoned that these locos were responsible for the high birth rate in the mill towns. The engines leaving in the morning, about five-thirty, used to blow the whistle just to let the manager know they were heading for the bush. And that used to wake everybody up. And the mill never used to start until eight o'clock. And the story was it was too early to get up and too late to go back to sleep.*

As a bush engine-driver, Roy Kelly sometimes wonders how he survived to describe the way he earned his living.

> *I think few people would believe the conditions under which bush railways worked at that time. To ride on the train. It's difficult to describe. It's like riding a bucking horse. You had to hang onto it and the ride was pretty rough. I would say, without fear of contradiction, that there were no lines anywhere rougher than what there was on log hauling on the bush tracks. You completely ignored all regulations. But they knew you were doing that. But you had to get the logs in otherwise the mills stopped. Wherever the timber was the line went. If you had the main*

Jarrah logs, c1920.

> line you had so many spur lines and it never made any difference how steep it was. You had to get the timber out!

On one occasion the engine crew had made room on the footplate for a distinguished visitor from the city, in his best business suit. Roy and his fireman had already warned him that the ride could be a little rough.

> And sure enough we were waiting for the other engine at a crossing and after we kicked off we were going through the crossing and the tender jumped off. And this visitor's on the side. He jumped on the side of this cutting. He hung on like on a ring-tailed possum and by the time we'd stopped jumping over the sleepers he was on the top of the bank looking at us and we never saw him after. We don't know how he got home. We was about nine mile out but he wouldn't come back on the loco.

There was a lot of forest to separate the bush workers, both from each other and from the mill towns, which were the focus of social activity. For Jack Thomson, places such as Pemberton and Shannon Mill were warm, vital centres of energy and life, if only by contrast with the isolated bush camps.

> You got pretty lonely out there, y'know, with the same old faces and you got sick of reading the labels on the jam tins. It was a real treat to go into a house where there was a woman, and, you know, the homely, womanly atmosphere, and a little child. As the eldest of a family of six I was fairly used to that sort of thing.

Jack, as a keen footballer, was drawn into the dances because they raised money for his club. From then on it became the most exciting recreation.

He learned to dance at a mill town ball, taught by three girls from Augusta. They didn't believe him when he said he didn't

Timber mill, Jarrahdale, c1910.

know how to, waltzed him onto the floor and danced with him right through until daylight.

> *It was a marvellous experience the dancing. Everybody brought their kids. There'd be babies and grandmothers and grandfathers there. And the old people generally sat down and talked. And they all brought blankets and things for the kids and plenty of food. They slept there and the band'd be going – or the old accordion.*

For Charlie's wife, Jessie Tozer, the dances were a great family and community occasion. Everybody baked, made biscuits and cakes for the ball, often serving four sessions of food as the mill towns danced Saturday night away.

Those weekly dances and the Saturday sport, more than most other activities, helped reinforce an already strong sense of community.

Jessie Coleman came from the city to a mill town and never regretted it.

> *The sense of community was outstanding. I couldn't call it anything else. Notably if anyone was sick or had sick children. There were always people on the doorstep to do their washing, their cleaning, look after their children, take care of them in every way. And I found this quite incredible after living in a city for all of my life until then.*

All the people I spoke to while recording 'Something Unique' had one thing in common. In different ways they all valued the forest environment. Today when the forest is under considerable pressure from the demands of industry, their thoughts are all the more worth recording.

Ron Meldrum, former forester:

> *The big trees, as we know them, six, seven, eight feet in*

Mill town, c1930.

diameter. We will never see them milled again, after the next few years, because it takes too long to produce them.

Kathleen Ffoulkes, a long-time mill town resident:

You feel that it's a living thing that has gone. You felt something was dying every time you saw a tree fall.

Charlie Tozer, after a lifetime of cutting timber:

I like tall trees but they're like anything else. They reach their maturity. We're the same and over we go! No, I love the trees, love the forest, but, as I say, they're put on the earth for a use and if we don't use them they're just going to fall down and rot! If you'd seen the timber I've seen in the bush, wasted, just blown over and left there.

And Ron Meldrum, a veteran tree faller:

You get in the middle, deep in the forest. And you look around you and you just can't imagine how the rest of the world can behave as it does.

(Based on the ABC Radio documentary broadcast in November 1983)

Hauling through the forest.

PICTORIAL REFERENCES

Cover	Battye Library ref. 4718P
4	Battye Library ref. 2890B/120
22	Battye Library ref. BA 352/37
25	Eastern Goldfields Historical Society ref. LR8
27	Battye Library ref. 4408P
29	Battye Library ref. 5979P
31	Battye Library ref. 5010P
33	Battye Library ref. 3184P
37	Battye Library ref. BA 352/35
39	Battye Library ref. 24402P, Royal Western Australian Historical Society
43	Eastern Goldfields Historical Society ref. 203/8
45	Battye Library ref. 4753P
46	Sr Eileen Heath
49	Battye Library ref. BA 368/4
51	Office of Aboriginal Affairs, New South Wales, ref. AR 8351
53	Australian Institute of Aboriginal and Torres Strait Islander Studies ref. N3524.9
59	West Australian Newspapers
61	Margaret Morgan
65	Margaret Morgan
67	Battye Library ref. BA 368/4
69	Battye Library ref. BA 368/4
71	Battye Library ref. 70684P
73	West Australian Newspapers
74	Battye Library ref. 29945P
77	Joan Fletcher
79	Battye Library ref. 4336B/132
81	George and Dorothy Brenton
83	Philip E M Blond

85   Peggy Adams
87   Dick Mumford
89   George and Dorothy Brenton
91   Battye Library ref. 4336B/123
93   Battye Library 2890B/82
95   Battye Library ref. 4739B/1
99   Joan Pascoe
100 Eastern Goldfields Historical Society ref.239/5
103 Museum of the Goldfields ref. 2610
105 Eastern Goldfields Historical Society ref. 222/18
109 Battye Library
113 Eastern Goldfields Historical Society ref. 222/6
115 West Australian Newspapers
117 Eastern Goldfields Historical Society ref. 222/17
119 Eastern Goldfields Historical Society ref. 239/1
121 Western Australian Museum ref. 8801/20/9
125 Battye Library
127 Western Australian Museum ref. 8801/19/16
128 Mirror Australian Telegraph Publications, Sydney
131 Richard Beilby
133 The Salvation Army, Melbourne
135 Richard Beilby
137 Joan Fletcher
139 The *Herald and Weekly Times*, Melbourne
141 West Australian Newspapers
143 The *Herald and Weekly Times*, Melbourne
145 Fremantle Society
147 Richard Beilby
151 Battye Library ref. 3728B/120
153 The *Herald and Weekly Times*, Melbourne
155 West Australian Newspapers
156 Battye Library ref. 29106P, Joy Mort Collection
159 Battye Library ref. 29107P, Joy Mort Collection
163 Battye Library ref. 72238P
165 Battye Library ref. BA 368/4
169 Battye Library ref. BA 368/4
171 Battye Library ref. 368/4F5.2
175 Battye Library ref. 29101P
177 Battye Library ref. 72230P
179 Battye Library

183	Margaret Morgan
185	Battye Library ref. 72252P
187	Battye Library ref. 29099P, Joy Mort Collection
188	Battye Library ref. 10638P
191	Battye Library ref. 7814P
193	Battye Library ref. BA 352/20
195	Dick Perry
197	Battye Library ref. BA 352/18
199	Battye Library ref. 1436P
205	Battye Library ref. BA 352/19
207	Battye Library ref. BA 533/335
209	Battye Library ref. 150P
211	Battye Library ref. 22022P
213	Battye Library ref. 307/402